An early photograph of Abraham Lincoln.

THE MYTH OF THE GREAT EMANCIPATOR
Abraham Lincoln's Views on Slavery and Race

by Greg Loren Durand

Institute for Southern Historical Review
Toccoa, Georgia

The Myth of the Great Emancipator
Abraham Lincoln's Views on Race and Slavery
by Greg Loren Durand

Published by
The Institute for Southern Historical Review
Post Office Box 2027 Toccoa, Georgia 30577
www.southernhistoricalreview.org

Cover and interior design by
Magnolia Graphic Design

Abraham Lincoln was not, above all other things, the liberator of the colored race. He never contemplated with any degree of substantiation the prospect of a free negro race living in the same country as a free white race.

— Roy Basler

I will say then that I am not, nor ever have been in favor of bringing about in any way the social and political equality of the white and black races – that I am not nor ever have been in favor of making voters or jurors of negroes, nor of qualifying them to hold office, nor to intermarry with white people; and I will say in addition to this that there is a physical difference between the white and black races which I believe will forever forbid the two races living together on terms of social and political equality.

— Abraham Lincoln

CONTENTS

CHAPTER ONE
"The White Man's President"

Most Americans today have an almost religious reverence for the memory of Abraham Lincoln, believing him to be the ideological predecessor to the 1960s civil rights icon, Martin Luther King, Jr. According to one writer, Lincoln "was a powerful statesman with a moral vision of where his country must go to preserve and enlarge the rights of all its people," and like Lincoln, King "was a world historical individual who embodied the essence of his age. . . . What King said and did carried on Lincoln's work and helped move America a long step closer to the realization of her ancient dream of equality for all."[1] So ingrained is this belief in the collective consciousness of the nation that it would be viewed as indecorous, if not outright heresy, to suggest that the man seated in the Greek-style temple on the Potomac was anything but the destroyer of slavery and harbinger of Negro equality. The inconvenient truth

---

1. Stephen B. Oates, *Builders of the Dream: Abraham Lincoln and Martin Luther King, Jr.* (Fort Wayne, Indiana: Lincoln Library and Museum, 1982), page 1.

about Lincoln, however, is that he "was not, above all other things, the liberator of the colored race. He never contemplated with any degree of substantiation the prospect of a free negro race living in the same country as a free white race."[2] Instead, his views on the Black man were typical of a member of the Border State laboring class: "Descended from the poor whites of a slave State, through many generations, he inherited the contempt, if not the hatred, held by that class for the negro. . . . [H]e could no more feel sympathy for that wretched race than he could for the horse he worked or the hog he killed."[3] Moreover, Lincoln "was sentimentally opposed to slavery, but he was afraid of freedom. He dreaded its effect on both races. He was opposed to slavery more because it was a public nuisance than because of its injustice to the oppressed black man, whose condition, he did not believe, would be greatly, if at all, benefitted by freedom."[4]

Even a cursory examination of Lincoln's speeches and correspondence will substantiate this assessment. Although he had previously made a few passing references to slavery, the bulk of his statements on the subject were made during the period beginning in the fall of 1854 to the end of his life. According to his own recollections, it was the Kansas-Nebraska Act which moved him to speak his

2. Roy Basler (editor), *Abraham Lincoln: His Speeches and Writings* (Cleveland, Ohio: The World Publishing Company, 1946), page 423.

3. Donn Piatt, *Memories of the Men Who Saved the Union* (New York: Belford, Clarke and Company, 1887), page 31.

4. John F. Hume, *The Abolitionists, Together With Personal Memories of the Struggle For Human Rights* (New York: G.P. Putnam's Sons, 1905), page 145.

mind publicly on the institution and its extension into the western Territories.[5] In his debate with Stephen Douglas at Peoria, Illinois on October 15, 1854, he said:

> When southern people tell us they are no more re-sponsible for the origin of slavery, than we; I acknowl-edge the fact. When it is said that the institution exists; and that it is very difficult to get rid of it, in any satisfactory way, I can understand and appreciate the saying. I surely will not blame them for not doing what I should not know how to do myself. If all earthly power were given me, I should not know what to do, as to the exist-ing institution. My first impulse would be to free all the slaves, and send them to Liberia, — to their own native land. But a moment's reflection would convince me, that whatever of high hope, (as I think there is) there may be in this, in the long run, its sudden execution is impossible. If they were all landed there in a day, they would all perish in the next ten days; and there are not surplus shipping and surplus money enough in the world to carry them there in many times ten days. What then? Free them all, and keep them among us as under-lings? Is it quite certain that this betters their condition? I think I would not hold one in slavery, at any rate; yet the point is not clear enough for me to denounce people upon. What next? Free them, and make them politically and socially, our equals? My own feelings will not ad-mit of this; and if mine would, we well know that those of the great mass of white people will not. Whether this feeling accords with justice and sound judgment, is not

5. Speech at Chicago, Illinois on July 10, 1858; Roy Basler (editor), *Collected Works of Abraham Lincoln* (New Brunswick, New Jersey: Rutgers University Press, 1953), Volume II, page 492.

the sole question, if indeed, it is any part of it. A universal feeling, whether well or ill founded, can not be safely
disregarded. We can not, then, make them equals. . . .

Let it not be said I am contending for the establishment of political and social equality between the whites
and blacks. I have already said the contrary.[6]

During his 1858 campaign against Douglas for a seat
in the United States Senate, Lincoln was accused of being
duplicitous on the subject of race, appearing to favor Negro
equality in the northern parts of the State in order to appeal
to the larger number of Abolitionists there, while express-
ing more moderate views in the southern counties where
"Black Republicanism" was generally reprobated.[7] Lincoln,
it was said, "has a fertile genius in devising language to
conceal his thoughts," and "he can trim his principals any
way in any section, so as to secure votes."[8] It may have
been true that Lincoln chose his words carefully, depending
on the perceived disposition of his audience, but his basic
position remained the same wherever he spoke. At Springfield on July 17, he said, "My declarations upon this subject
of negro slavery may be misrepresented, but cannot be
misunderstood. I have said that I do not understand the
Declaration [of Independence] to mean that all men were

6. Basler, *Collected Works of Lincoln*, Volume II, pages 255-256, 267.

7. Stephen Douglas appears to have been the originator of the term
"Black Republican" during a speech delivered on October 3, 1854 at
the Illinois State Agricultural Fair (reported by the *Missouri Republican*,
October 6, 1854).

8. Marion Mills Miller and Francis Bicknell Carpenter (editors), *The
Works of Abraham Lincoln: Speeches and Debates, 1858-1859* (New York:
C.S. Hammond and Company, 1907), pages 79, 108.

created equal in all respects. . . . Certainly the negro is not our equal in color – perhaps not in many other respects. . . ."[9] During his debate with Douglas at Ottawa on August 21, he said:

> . . . [T]his is the true complexion of all I have ever said in regard to the institution of slavery and the black race. This is the whole of it, and anything that argues me into his idea of perfect social and political equality with the negro, is but a specious and fantastic arrangement of words, by which a man can prove a horse chestnut to be a chestnut horse. I will say here, while upon this subject, that I have no purpose directly or indirectly to interfere with the institution of slavery in the States where it exists. I believe I have no lawful right to do so, and I have no inclination to do so. I have no purpose to introduce political and social equality between the white and the black races. There is a physical difference be-tween the two, which in my judgment will probably forever forbid their living together upon the footing of perfect equality, and inasmuch as it becomes a necessity that there must be a difference, I, as well as Judge Douglas, am in favor of the race to which I belong, hav-ing the superior position. I have never said anything to the contrary.[10]

On September 18, he elaborated on this statement at Charleston, in the eastern part of the State:

> While I was at the hotel to-day an elderly gentleman

9. Basler, *Collected Works of Lincoln*, Volume II, page 520.

10. Basler, ibid., Volume III, page 16.

called upon me to know whether I was really in favor of producing a perfect equality between the negroes and white people. While I had not proposed to myself on this occasion to say much on that subject, yet as the question was asked me I thought I would occupy perhaps five minutes in saying something in regard to it. I will say then that I am not, nor ever have been in favor of bringing about in any way the social and political equality of the white and black races – that I am not nor ever have been in favor of making voters or jurors of negroes, nor of qualifying them to hold office, nor to intermarry with white people; and I will say in addition to this that there is a physical difference between the white and black races which I believe will forever forbid the two races living together on terms of social and political equality. And inasmuch as they cannot so live, while they do remain together there must be the position of the superior and the inferior, and I as much as any other man am in favor of having the superior position assigned to the white race.[11]

When Douglas accused him of refusing to address the issue of Negro citizenship, Lincoln said, "I tell [Judge Douglas] very frankly that I am not in favor of negro citizenship. . . . Now my opinion is that the different States have the power to make a negro a citizen under the Constitution of the United States if they choose. . . . If the State of Illinois had that power I should be opposed to the exercise of it. That is all I have to say about it."[12] This was nothing new, for he had previously stated his conviction that "this

11. Basler, ibid., pages 145-146.
12. Basler, ibid., page 179.

government was made for the white people and not for the negroes,"[13] and he had never objected to any of the legislation in his State which barred Blacks from voting or holding office.

Lincoln's private views were no different than those he expressed in public. In an October 18, 1858 letter to fellow Illinois politician, James N. Brown, he wrote, "I do not perceive how I can express myself more plainly than I have done in the foregoing extracts. In four of them I have expressly disclaimed all intention to bring about social and political equality between the white and black races, and, in all the rest, I have done the same thing by clear implication."[14] In some fragments of speech notes written in September of 1859 are found these words: "Negro equality. Fudge!! How long in the Government of a God great enough to make and maintain this universe, shall there continue to be knaves to vend and fools to gulp, so low a piece of demagoguism as this?"[15]

It is important to remember that political posturing is not just a modern phenomenon; efforts to "smear" the opposing party or candidate with exaggerations and even outright falsehoods, resulting in rebuttals and counterattacks from the intended target, were as common in the Nineteenth Century as they are now. Each party strove to portray themselves in the best possible light, and their opponent in the worst, all designed to play upon the perceived fears or desires of the general public. One of the

13. Basler, ibid., Volume II, page 281.

14. Basler, ibid., Volume III, page 399.

15. Basler, ibid., page 328.

greatest fears of the Northern people at that time was that their States would be overrun with Blacks and any movement toward abolition was viewed as the precursor to that end. This is precisely the point emphasized by the Northern Democrats. When the Democratic press in Illinois vigorously opposed him with the claim, "Lincoln says that the negro is your equal," and, "A vote for the Republican candidate is a vote to crowd White laborers out of, and bring Negroes into the city,"[16] the Republican response was immediate and unequivocal: "Nigger equality is as false against Lincoln as the charge of *Toryism* & *Abolitionism* was against Clay" (emphasis in original).[17] The same charges of "Black Republicanism" were again raised by the Democrats in 1860 when Lincoln was nominated as the Republican presidential candidate. The editors of the *New York Herald* insisted that, once in control of both the White House and Congress, Lincoln and the Republicans would abolish slavery in the South in order to "establish a new social policy in this country – the policy of an equalization of the white and black races." The "grand object" of the Republican party, according to the *Herald*, was racial "amalgamation."[18] Again, the Republican press responded, often in lengthy editorials such as the following:

> We have denied this and we deny it again. There are men in the Northern States who uphold and advocate that doctrine, — but they are few in number and are not

16. "Lincoln on the 'Equality' of the Races," *Daily Illinois State Journal*, October 8, 1858.

17. *Illinois State Journal*, October 5, 1858.

18. *New York Herald*, September 5 and 19, 1860.

increasing. The Republican party, as such, has never been committed to it. . . .

The field for carrying this principle into effect is in State legislation. Yet in how many of those States in which the Republicans have full political sway, have negroes been placed on a footing of complete political equality with whites? . . . Before anything can be done by the North for Southern slaves, they must be set free, — and then they fall at once into the category of "free negroes" whom the North . . . absolutely and thoroughly despise. Pray how is the doctrine of negro equality to be "forced upon the South" by the Republicans, when they scout and scorn it for the free negroes of the North?

In point of fact, the Republicans . . . entertain very much the same feeling towards the negroes as other sensible white men, North and South. . . . They recognize their degradation — their mental, social and political inferiority to the whites, as a fact . . . and they have not the slightest disposition to give them authority or control over social movements or the development of social civilization. It is a great mistake, moreover, to suppose that as a party the Republicans are in favor of emancipating the slaves. . . .

We fear, indeed, that our Southern brethren overrate the philanthropy of the Republicans towards the negroes. . . . We do not believe they have any more love of the negro . . . than the rest of mankind, North and South. Whenever the matter comes to be practically tested, we presume it will be discovered to be pretty thoroughly a white man's party . . . looking mainly and steadily to the advancement of the interests, the development of the character and the promotion of the welfare and happiness of the great mass of our white American society. So far as their apprehensions that the Republicans will introduce an era of negro equality are real, our Southern friends may dismiss them at once.[19]

During a Republican convention at the city hall in Brooklyn on June 27, 1860, Francis P. Blair, a Senator from Missouri, similarly complained to the assembled crowd "that the Republicans were called 'Black,' because their aim was to dignify free white labor, and sustain white men: and the Democracy called themselves white because they wished to cover the country with niggers, to the exclusion of white men." The audience was urged to "put the Government into the hands of Lincoln. He will respect the rights of the whites."[20]

On September 4, the *New York Times* noted that, despite the persistent efforts of the Democrats to paint him as a radical, "It begins to be universally seen and felt, that Mr. Lincoln's position is eminently conservative, and that his election will by no means involve a triumph of the ultra Anti-Slavery element of the Northern and Eastern States." It was also noted that a "good many of the more zealous" Abolitionists had grown "disgusted with the conservative tendencies of the Republican Party" and were calling for

---

19. "The Republicans and the Doctrine of Negro Equality," *New York Times*, August 28, 1860, page 4. This quotation has been edited to conserve space. The original may be read online in its entirety at www.nytimes.com/1860/08/28/archives/the-republicans-and-the-doctrine-of-negro-equality.html

20. "Republican Ratification Meeting in Brooklyn," ibid., June 28, 1860, page 1. Francis Blair's brother was Montgomery Blair, Lincoln's Postmaster-General.

the organization of their own party.[21] Indeed, Lincoln's views were completely in line with the official position of the Republican party on slavery and race. While he personally disliked slavery and favored its gradual and peaceful termination throughout Union,[22] he was certainly not an Abolitionist. He repeatedly acknowledged that the institution was protected by the Constitution and that the Federal Government was prevented by that document from legislating against slavery within any of the States where it already existed: "The Congress of the United States has no power, under the constitution, to interfere with the institution of slavery in the different states;"[23] and, "I say that we must not interfere with the institution of slavery in the states where it exists, because the constitution forbids it, and the general welfare does not require us to do so."[24] Throughout his political career, Lincoln never wavered in his denial that "the power of emancipation is in the Federal Government,"[25] not even when he issued his celebrated, but often misinterpreted, Emancipation Proclamation. He also condemned efforts by private individuals or organi-

---

21. "Lincoln and Slavery: Conservatism of the Republican Candidate, ibid., September 4, 1860.

22. Basler, *Collected Works of Lincoln*, Volume III, pages 370, 440. In his annual address to Congress on December 1, 1862, Lincoln proposed a constitutional amendment that would give the States the choice of abolishing slavery immediately or in degrees over a span of 38 years — either option with compensation from the Federal Government for their loss in slave property value (ibid., Volume V, page 531).

23. Basler, ibid., Volume I, page 75.

24. Basler, ibid., Volume III, page 460.

25. Basler, ibid., page 541.

zations to create disturbances in the South on the subject: "I have said a hundred times, and I have now no inclination to take it back, that I believe there is no right, and ought to be no inclination in the people of the free States to enter into the slave States, and interfere with the question of slavery at all."[26]

Like the majority of his Republican colleagues, Lincoln's public opposition to the institution applied only to its extension into the Territories, which he strongly believed should be reserved for White laborers. In a speech on the Kansas-Nebraska Act, delivered on October 16, 1854 in Peoria, Illinois, he said, "I wish to make and to keep the distinction between the existing institution, and the extension of it, so broad, and so clear, that no honest man can misunderstand me, and no dishonest one, successfully misrepresent me. . . . The whole nation is interested that the best use be made of these Territories. We want them for homes of free white people. This they cannot be, to any considerable extent, if slavery shall be planted within them."[27] Four years later, he said much the same thing in a speech at Alton, Illinois on October 15, 1858: "Now irrespective of the moral aspect of this question as to whether there is a right or wrong in enslaving a negro, I am still in favor of our new Territories being in such a condition that white men may find a home . . . where they can settle upon new soil and better their condition in life. I am in favor of this not merely . . . for our own people who are born amongst us, but as an outlet for free

26. Basler, ibid., Volume II, page 492.
27. Basler, ibid., pages 248, 268.

white people everywhere, the world over. . . ."[28]

In discussing his views on slavery, Lincoln was always very careful not to allow himself to be "tarred with the abolitionist brush."[29] He viewed the Abolitionists as "a disturbing element,"[30] and often spoke of them "in terms of contempt and derision"[31] for their "self righteousness" and "petulance and vicious fretfulness."[32] In a set of resolutions submitted to the Illinois legislature on March 3, 1837, he stated that, while "the institution of slavery is founded on both injustice and bad policy," the spread of Abolitionism "tends rather to increase than to abate its evils."[33] In his July 6, 1852 eulogy of his "beau ideal of a statesman," Henry Clay,[34] Lincoln advocated "gradual emancipation" over against outright abolition, insisting that slavery could not be "at *once* eradicated, without producing a greater evil, even to the cause of human liberty itself" (emphasis in original). In contrast, he criticized those who "would shiver into fragments the Union of these States; tear to tatters its now venerated constitution; and even burn the last copy of the Bible, rather than slavery should continue a single hour," and approved of the fact that they "together

---

28. Basler, ibid., Volume III, page 312.

29. Basler, *Lincoln: Speeches and Writings*, page 344.

30. Piatt, *Men Who Saved the Union*, page 30.

31. Michael Burlingame and John R. Turner (editors), *Inside Lincoln's White House: The Complete Civil War Diary of John Hay* (Carbondale, Illinois: Southern Illinois University Press, 1997), page 322.

32. William D. Kelley, *Lincoln and Stanton* (New York: G. P. Putnam's Sons, 1885), page 86.

33. Basler, *Collected W.orks of Lincoln*, Volume I, page 75.

34. Basler, ibid., Volume III, page 29.

with all their more halting sympathisers, have received, and are receiving their just execration."[35] In his February 27, 1860 address at the Cooper Institute in New York, he ridiculed John Brown's failed attempt at Harper's Ferry to incite a widespread slave insurrection as "so absurd that the slaves, with all their ignorance, saw plainly enough it could not succeed," and describing its mastermind as "an enthusiast [who] broods over the oppression of a people till he fancies himself commissioned by Heaven to liberate them."[36] He did not believe that "in the present state of things in the United States . . . a general, or even a very extensive slave insurrection, is possible," and one of the reasons he gave for this opinion further distinguished him from the Northern radicals: "Much is said by Southern people about the affection of slaves for their masters and mistresses; and a part of it, at least, is true. A plot for an uprising could scarcely be devised and communicated to twenty individuals before some one of them, to save the life of a favorite master or mistress, would divulge it."[37]

During his presidency, Lincoln was constantly har-

---

35. Basler, ibid., Volume II, page 130. Lincoln was here referring to radicals such as William Lloyd Garrison, who condemned the Union as "a covenant with death and an agreement with hell" (*The Liberator*, Volume XXV, Number 24, June 15, 1855) and publicly burned a copy of the Constitution at an Abolitionist rally in 1854, and Wendell Phillips, who insisted that the Constitution was a "pro-slavery compact" which "ought to be immediately annulled" and that "to continue this disastrous alliance [Union] longer is madness" (*The Constitution a Pro-Slavery Compact* [New York: American Anti-Slavery Society, 1856], page 9).

36. Basler, *Collected Works of Lincoln*, Volume III, page 541.

37. Basler, ibid., page 540.

rassed by the Abolitionist leaders in his own party for his refusal to conform his war policy to their demands. He once referred to these men as "almost fiendish" and, being "fully aware that they would strike him at once, if they durst,"[38] one of the ways he attempted to control them was to appoint them to positions in his cabinet and other key positions in the Government.[39] Foremost among these was the ambitious and pugnacious Salmon P. Chase, whom Lincoln referred to on one occasion as a "maggot,"[40] and yet appointed Secretary of the Treasury and later as Chief Justice of the Supreme Court. Lincoln understood the necessity of uniting the conservatives and radicals within the party, but his efforts to conciliate the two factions should not be taken as agreement with the latter. He was adept at manipulating his opponents for his own purposes, and "[r]egardless of their position on the political spectrum, most came away persuaded that Lincoln was on their side."[41]

It is doubtful that any of his contemporaries would have recognized the real Lincoln in the great anti-slavery crusader of modern lore. According to the outspoken Wen-

---

38. Howard K. Beale (editor), *The Diary of Edward Bates, 1859-1866* (Washington, D. C.: Government Printing Office, 1933), page 333; entry for February 13, 1864.

39. Doris Kearns Goodwin, *Team of Rivals: The Political Genius of Abraham Lincoln* (New York: Simon and Schuster, 2005).

40. Thurlow Weed, letter to John Bigelow, December 13, 1863; John Bigelow, *Retrospections of an Active Life* (New York: The Baker and Taylor Company, 1909), Volume II, page 110.

41. Eric Foner, *The Fiery Trial: Abraham Lincoln and American Slavery* (New York: W. Norton and Company, 2010), page 193.

dell Phillips, he was "not an Abolitionist [and] hardly an Anti-Slavery man," but was a mere "pawn on the political chessboard" that could "soon [be] change[d] for knight, bishop or queen, and sweep the board."[42] Lincoln expert Roy Basler noted that he "barely mentioned slavery before 1854"[43] — the year the Republican party was born. There were other issues, specifically "internal improvements, protective tariffs, and centralized banking" (Henry Clay's "American System"), to which he was vastly more committed than a mere opposition to the extension of slavery.[44] In fact, the latter was viewed by him and those who nominated him as a means to an end: the protection of the labor and racial purity of the White man. It cannot be doubted that Lincoln was a White nationalist, as were most of his political colleagues, and that he died "with the same basic views on black-white relations that he had held tenaciously throughout his public life."[45]

At the dedication of the Freedmen's Monument in Washington, D.C. on April 14, 1876, Frederick Douglass, summarized Lincoln's views as follows:

---

42. Speech delivered at Tremont Temple in Boston on November 7, 1860; *Speeches, Lectures, and Letters by Wendell Phillips* (Boston: Lee and Shepard, 1894), Volume I, page 294.

43. Basler, *Lincoln: Speeches and Writings*, page 23.

44. Robert W. Johannsen, *Lincoln, the South, and Slavery* (Baton Rouge: Louisiana State University Press, 1991), page 14; see also Reinhard H. Luthin, "Abraham Lincoln and the Tariff," *The American Historical Review* (July, 1944), Volume XLIX, Number 4.

45. George M. Frederickson, "A Man But Not a Brother: Abraham Lincoln and Racial Equality," *The Journal of Southern History*, Volume XLI, Number 1 (February, 1975), page 58.

We fully comprehend the relation of Abraham Lincoln both to ourselves and to the white people of the United States. . . . It must be admitted, truth compels me to admit, even here in the presence of the monument we have erected to his memory, Abraham Lincoln was not, in the fullest sense of the word, either our man or our model. In his interests, in his associations, in his habits of thought, and in his prejudices, he was a white man.

He was preeminently the white man's President, entirely devoted to the welfare of white men. He was ready and willing at any time during the first years of his administration to deny, postpone, and sacrifice the rights of humanity in the coloured people to promote the welfare of the white people of this country. In all his education and feeling he was an American of the Americans. He came into the Presidential chair upon one principal alone, namely, opposition to the extension of slavery. His arguments in furtherance of this policy had then motive and mainspring in his patriotic devotion to the interests of his own race. To protect, defend, and perpetuate slavery in the States where it existed, Abraham Lincoln was not less ready than any other President to draw the sword of the nation. He was ready to execute all the supposed constitutional guarantees of the United States Constitution in favour of the slave system anywhere inside the slave States. He was willing to pursue, recapture, and send back the fugitive slave to his master, and to suppress a slave rising to his master for liberty, though his guilty master were already in arms against the Government. The race to which we belong were not the special objects of his consideration.[46]

---

46. Frederick Douglass, *The Life and Times of Frederick Douglass* (London: Christian Age Office, 1882), page 372.

CHAPTER TWO
Lincoln's Support of Negro Colonization

As already shown, Abraham Lincoln's opposition to slavery was primarily motivated by a concern for its negative effect on White labor and property, as well as a belief that, in associating together, "the inferior race bears the superior down."[1] Consequently, the only way the great American experiment in free White government could ultimately succeed was through the removal and colonization of the Negroes. As the consummate politician, Lincoln often did and said what was politically expedient at the moment. However, in his advocacy for colonization he remained entirely consistent. In fact, the subject was discussed in no less than eight of his major public speeches. On July 6, 1852, he referred to Henry Clay's work to "rid our country of a useless and pernicious, if not dangerous

---

1. Speech at Chicago on July 10, 1858; Basler, *Collected Works of Lincoln*, Volume II, page 498. Lincoln was here paraphrasing his debate opponent, Stephen Douglas, but his following words show that he did not disagree with him on this point: "Why, Judge, if we do not let them get together in the Territories they won't mix there."

portion of the population"[2] as "more valuable" than any of his other labors.[3] In an address delivered on October 16, 1854 at Peoria, Illinois, he stated, "If all earthly power were given me, I should not know what to do as to the existing institution [of slavery]. My first impulse would be to free all the slaves, and send them to Liberia – to their own native land."[4] On June 26, 1857, he continued, "Such separation, if ever effected at all, must be effected by colonization. . . . Let us be brought to believe it is morally right, and at the same time favorable to, or at least not against, our interest to transfer the African to his native clime, and we shall find a way to do it, however great the task may be."[5] The following year, on July 17, he told an audience at his hometown of Springfield, Illinois, "What I would most desire would be the separation of the white and black races."[6]

One of Lincoln's earliest acts as President was to appoint Elisha O. Crosby of New York as United States Minister to Guatemala in March of 1861 and send him on a secret mission to discuss a colonization plan with dictator Rafael Carrera.[7] On April 10, Lincoln also met with Ambrose W. Thompson, the head of the Chiriquí Improvement

---

2. James F. Hopkins (editor), *The Papers of Henry Clay: The Rising Statesman 1815-1820* (Lexington, Kentucky: University of Kentucky Press, 1961), Volume II, page 264.

3. Basler, *Collected Works of Lincoln*, Volume II, page 132.

4. Basler, ibid., page 256.

5. Basler, ibid., page 409.

6. Basler, ibid., page 521.

7. Charles A. Barker (editor), *Memoirs of Elisha Oliver Crosby: Reminiscences of California and Guatemala From 1849 to 1864* (San Marino, California: Huntington Library, 1945), page 87.

Association, to create a 10,000 acre colony in Panama where emancipated slaves could be sent to mine coal for the Navy.[8] Three members of his cabinet — Interior Secretary Caleb Smith, Postmaster General Montgomery Blair, and Attorney General Edward Bates — supported this plan. Henceforth, Lincoln spoke on this subject so frequently that he earned the displeasure of several prominent free Blacks, most notably Frederick Douglass, who criticized the President's "ever increasing passion for making himself appear silly and ridiculous" for suggesting that Black people leave the country of their birth: "Mr. Lincoln assumes the language and arguments of an itinerant Colonization lecturer, showing all his inconsistencies, his pride of race and blood, his contempt for Negroes and his canting hypocrisy."[9] In his first annual address to Congress on December 3, 1861, Lincoln proposed a plan in which the Government would accept payment in slaves in lieu of direct taxes, and that such slaves be declared free and then colonized "at some place or places in a climate congenial to them." He also suggested that "the free colored people already in the United States" be included in the colonization endeavor.[10] On April 16, 1862 he again

---

8. Paul J. Scheips, "Lincoln and the Chiriqui Colonization Project," *The Journal of Negro History*, Volume XXXVII, Number 4 (October, 1952), pages 418-453; Gideon Welles, *Diary of Gideon Welles, Secretary of the Navy Under Lincoln and Johnson* (Boston: Houghton Mifflin Company, 1911), Volume I, page 150.

9. *Douglass' Monthly*, September 1862; Philip S. Foner (editor), *The Life and Writings of Frederick Douglass* (New York: International Publishers, 1950), Volume III, page 270.

10. Basler, *Collected Works of Lincoln*, Volume V, pages 35-54.

discussed his views on colonization with Congress,[11] and further on July 12: "Room in South America may be obtained cheaply and in abundance, and when numbers shall be large enough to be company and encouragement to one another, the freed people will not be so reluctant to go."[12]

On August 14, 1862, Lincoln invited five Negro ministers to the White House, which was the first time any such delegation had entered the Executive Mansion to discuss matters of public policy. Despite the fact that these men were highly respected members of the free Black elite of the city with strong ties to local religious and civic associations, Lincoln made it clear that the meeting was intended to be a one-sided presentation of his views on colonization:

> Why . . . should people of your race be colonized, and where? Why should they leave this country? This is, perhaps, the first question for proper consideration. You and we are different races. We have between us a broader difference than exists between almost any other two races. Whether it is right or wrong I need not discuss, but this physical difference is a great disadvantage to us both, as I think your race suffers very greatly, many of them, by living among us, while ours suffers from your presence. In a word we suffer on each side. If this be admitted, it affords a reason at least why we should be separated.
>
> You are freemen I suppose. Perhaps you have long been free, or all your lives. Your race is suffering, in my judgment, the greatest wrong inflicted on any people. But

---

11. Basler, ibid., page 192.
12. Basler, ibid., page 318.

even when you cease to be slaves, you are yet far removed from being placed on an equality with the white race. You are cut off from many of the advantages which the other race enjoys. . . . The aspiration of men is to enjoy equality with the best when free, but on this broad continent, not a single man of your race is made the equal of a single man of ours. Go where you are treated the best, and the ban is still upon you.

I believe in its [slavery's] general evil effects on the white race. See our present condition – the country engaged in war – and then consider what we know to be the truth. But for your race among us there could not be war, although many men engaged on either side do not care for you one way or the other. . . . It is better for us both therefore to be separated. . . .[13]

In his preliminary draft of the Emancipation Proclamation on September 22, Lincoln announced, "[I]t is my purpose . . . to again recommend . . . that the effort to colonize persons of African descent with their consent upon this continent or elsewhere . . . will be continued."[14] At the urging of some in his cabinet, Lincoln removed this passage from the final draft of the proclamation lest it further alienate the Abolitionists in the Republican party who were already displeased with his tardiness in abolishing slavery. As much as he despised these men, Lincoln knew he would need their votes in his bid for re-election in 1864. However, colonization was still very much on his mind. In his second

---

13. Basler, ibid., pages 371-372.

14. *Statutes at Large, Treaties, and Proclamations of the United States of America* (Boston: Little, Brown and Company 1863), Volume XII, pages 1267–1268.

annual address to Congress on December 1, 1862, he stated, "I cannot make it better known than it already is, that I strongly favor colonization." He suggested Liberia or Haiti as possible destinations for the emigrants, although he admitted that the objects of his attention "do not seem so willing to migrate to those countries as to others. . . ."[15] On December 31 (one day before the Emancipation Proclamation went into effect), Lincoln signed a contract for the colonization of 5,000 freedmen on Île à Vache (Cow Island), a tiny uninhabited island off the southern coast of Haiti,[16] and he also sent letters to several countries in Central America inquiring as to their interest in receiving Negroes from the United States.[17] In early 1863, he discussed a plan with Register of the Treasury Lucius Chittenden "to remove the whole colored race of the slave States into Texas."[18] As always, the motive for colonization was to protect Whites against competition from either slave or free Black labor: "With deportation, even to a limited extent, enhanced wages to white labor is mathematically certain. Labor is like any other commodity in the market — increase the demand for it, and you increase the

---

15. Basler, *Collected Works of Lincoln*, Volume V, page 534.

16. Basler, ibid., Volume VI, pages 41-42. This poorly planned venture ended in utter disaster. None of the food or housing promised the 453 emigrants was ever provided, and they had to fend for themselves, resulting in the deaths of many of them from exposure, starvation, and disease within one year of landing (Phillip W. Magness, "The Île à Vache: From Hope to Disaster," *New York Times*, April 12, 2013).

17. Benjamin A. Quarles, *Lincoln and the Negro* (New York: Oxford University Press, 1962), pages 111-117.

18. Lucius E. Chittenden, *Recollections of President Lincoln and His Administration* (New York: Harper and Brothers, 1891), page 337.

price of it. Reduce the supply of black labor, by colonizing the black laborer out of the country, and, by precisely so much, you increase the demand for, and wages of, white labor."[19]

As the war dragged on, Lincoln's attention was diverted to more pressing military and civil matters, but once Union victory was assured, his mind returned again to his pet project of colonization where it remained right up to the time of his death. In fact, on April 11, 1865, he was making plans with General Benjamin Butler to ship the former slaves down to Panama to dig the canal. His unmistakable opinion was that the presence of the Black race in America would forever be the source of sectional strife: "I can hardly believe that the South and North can live in peace, unless we can get rid of the negroes. Certainly they cannot if we don't get rid of the negroes whom we have armed and disciplined and who have fought with us. . . . I believe that it would be better to export them all to some fertile country with a good climate, which they can have to themselves."[20] Had it not been for the fatal encounter with John Wilkes Booth at Ford's Theater three days later, there can be little doubt that Lincoln's role in Black American history would have been quite different.

Few were in a better position to know Lincoln's mind on this subject than his own bodyguard, Ward Lamon, and

19. Basler, *Collected Works of Lincoln*, Volume V, page 535.

20. Benjamin F. Butler, *Butler's Book* (Boston: A. M. Thayer and Company, 1892), Volume II, page 903. For more information, see Phillip W. Magness and Sebastian N. Page, *Colonization After Emancipation: Lincoln and the Movement for Black Resettlement* (Columbia, Missouri: University of Missouri Press, 2011).

his words are a fitting conclusion to this chapter:

> None of his public acts, either before or after he became President, exhibits any special tenderness for the African race, or any extraordinary commiseration of their lot. On the contrary, he invariably, in words and deeds, postponed the interests of the blacks to the interests of the whites, and expressly subordinated the one to the other. When he was compelled, by what he deemed an overruling necessity, founded on both military and political considerations, to declare the freedom of the public enemy's slaves, he did so with avowed reluctance, and took pains to have it understood that his resolution was in no wise affected by sentiment. He never at any time favored the admission of negroes into the body of electors, in his own State or in the States of the South. He claimed that those who were incidentally liberated by the Federal arms were poor spirited, lazy, and slothful; that they could be made soldiers only by force, and willing laborers not at all; that they seemed to have no interest in the cause of their own race, but were as docile in the service of the Rebellion as the mules that ploughed the fields or drew the baggage-trains; and, as a people, were useful only to those who were at the same time their masters and the foes of those who sought their good. With such views honestly formed, it is no wonder that he longed to see them transported to Hayti, Central America, Africa, or anywhere, so that they might in no event, and in no way, participate in the government of his country. Accordingly, he was, from the beginning, as earnest a colonizationist as Mr. Clay, and, even during his Presidency, zealously and persistently devised schemes for the deportation of the negroes, which the latter deemed cruel and atrocious in

the extreme. He believed, with his rival, that this was purely a "white man's government;" but he would have been perfectly willing to share its blessings with the black man, had he not been very certain that the blessings would disappear when divided with such a partner. He was no Abolitionist in the popular sense; did not want to break over the safeguards of the Constitution to interfere with slavery where it had a lawful existence; but, wherever his power rightfully extended, he was anxious that the negro should be protected, just as women and children and unnaturalized men are protected, in life, limb, property, reputation, and every thing that nature or law makes sacred. But this was all: he had no notion of extending to the negro the privilege of governing him and other white men, by making him an elector. That was a political trust, an office to be exercised only by the superior race.

It was therefore as a white man, and in the interests of white men, that he threw himself into the struggle to keep the blacks out of the Territories. He did not want them there either as slaves or freemen; but he wanted them less as slaves than as freemen.[21]

---

21. Ward Hill Lamon, *The Life of Abraham Lincoln: From His Birth to His Inauguration as President* (Boston: James R. Osgood and Company, 1872), pages 344-346.

CHAPTER THREE
Northern Anti-Black Prejudice

Abraham Lincoln's actual views on slavery and race were so out of line with the commonly accepted myth of the "Great Emancipator" that the historical evidence is often ignored or openly denied. While he would stand very little chance of being elected in today's politically-correct environment, his beliefs were not considered at all controversial at the time, not even among his fellow Northerners. According to one British observer, free Blacks throughout the North had always been "treated like lepers."[1] The biographers of William Lloyd Garrison noted that "the free colored people were looked upon as an inferior caste to whom their liberty was a curse, and their lot worse than that of the slaves. . . ." Throughout the North, there was a spirit which "either by statute or custom, denied to a dark skin, civil, social and educational

---

1. James Spence, "The American Republic: Resurrection Through Dissolution," *Northern British Review*, Number LXXXI, February 1862, page 240.

equality. . . ."[2] Negroes were typically viewed as "a depraved and inferior race which must be kept in its proper place in a white man's society."[3] Even in the absence of slavery, they were subjected to "a mental and moral subordination and inferiority" from which "no legislative act could free them. . . ."[4]

That free Blacks in the North were traditionally denied the same civil rights as Whites is a matter of record. For example, when drafting a constitution in preparation for admission to the Union, the Ohio convention, composed mainly of New Englanders, determined that "people of color" were not to be considered as parties and therefore should have no part in the administration of the new State government.[5] On January 5, 1804, the State legislature passed a law requiring Blacks to produce certificates of their freedom from a Court of Record and execute bonds not to become charges upon the counties in which they settled. Any White citizen discovered to have hired an unregistered Negro was subject to a $50 fine.[6] In 1831, the Ohio supreme court declared that "color alone is sufficient

2. Wendell Phillips Garrison and Francis Jackson Garrison, *William Lloyd Garrison, 1805-1870* (Boston, Massachusetts: Houghton, Mifflin Company, 1894), Volume I, pages 253-254.

3. Leon F. Litwack, *North of Slavery: The Negro in the Free States, 1790-1860* (Chicago, Illinois: University of Chicago Press, 1961), page viii.

4. John M. Duncan, *Travels Through Part of the United States and Canada in 1818 and 1819* (New York: W. B. Gilley, 1823), Volume I, page 60.

5. Jacob Burnet, *Notes on the Early Settlement of the North-Western Territory* (Cincinnati, Ohio: Derby, Bradley and Company, 1847), page 355.

6. 2 Ohio Laws 63; George W. Williams, *History of the Negro Race in America From 1619 to 1880* (New York: G. P. Putnam's Sons, 1885), Volume II, pages 111-119.

to indicate a negro's inability to testify against a white man,"[7] and in 1842, the court reiterated the State's original maxim: "It has always been admitted that our political institutions embrace the white population only. Persons of color were not recognized as having any political existence; they had no agency in our political organizations, and possessed no political rights under it."[8] One Ohio Congressman spoke for the majority of his constituents when he said, "I sympathize with [the Negroes] deeply, but I have no sympathy for them in a common residence with the white race. God has ordained, and no human law can contravene the ordinance, that the two races shall be separate and distinct. . . . I will vote against any measure that has a tendency to prolong their common residence in this Confederacy, or any portion of it."[9]

On February 10, 1831, the legislature of Indiana enacted similar restrictions to those in Ohio. Blacks were denied the right to vote, barred from service in the militia, could not testify in court cases involving Whites, and their children were not allowed to attend the public schools. The required $500 bond[10] was an effective deterrent to the vast majority of potential Negro immigrants, and as a result, Blacks rarely constituted more than one percent of the antebellum population.[11] Nevertheless, their presence in the State was

---

7. *Calvin v. Carter* (1831), 4 Ohio Rep., 386.

8. *Thatcher vs. Hawk* (1842), 4 Ohio Rep., 351.

9. Litwack, *North of Slavery*, page 49.

10. *The Revised Laws of Indiana* (Indianapolis, Indiana: Douglass and Maguire, 1831), pages 375-376.

11. Emma Lou Thornbrough, *The Negro in Indiana: A Study of a Minority* (Indianapolis, Indiana: Indiana Historical Bureau, 1957), pages 541-542.

a predominant topic of discussion during the constitutional convention of 1850. On October 28, Democrat delegate James G. Read emphasized the need "to prohibit the immigration of negroes to the State, to give no encouragement to those that are here that they can ever enjoy equal social or political privileges, and keep the State for ourselves and our descendants."[12] Whig delegate Alexander C. Stevenson likewise argued that it was "highly impolitic for a refined and superior class to keep in their midst an uncultivated, a degraded, and inferior race," and that any attempt to integrate the two races into a common society would prove "not to be elevation of the degraded, but the deterioration, the lowering, of the better class, towards the standard of the inferior class."[13] Other delegates were even more severe in their dislike of Negroes: "The race was cursed, and it was declared that they should be the servants of servants. That curse has never been removed. We cannot, therefore, be charged with inhumanity in preventing our State from being overrun with these vermin – for I say they are vermin, and I know it;"[14] and, "[I]f we are to be divided one against another, and our brightest prospects of the future blasted by the introduction among us of these beings — I would say . . . in all sincerity, and without any hard feelings toward them — that it would be better to kill them off at once, if there is no other way to get rid of them. We have not come to that point yet with the blacks,

---

12. *Report of the Debates and Proceedings of the Convention for the Revision of the Constitution of the State of Indiana, 1850* (Indianapolis, Indiana: A. H. Brown, 1850), Volume I, page 247.

13. Ibid., page 251.

14. Ibid., page 584.

but we know how the Puritans did with the Indians, who were infinitely more magnanimous and less impudent than this colored race."[15]

This anti-Black attitude was, to varying degrees, evident across party lines in the convention. Consequently, with the adoption of the 1851 constitution, Blacks and Mulattoes were entirely prohibited entry or settlement into the Hoosier State and a fine of "not less than ten dollars, nor more than five hundred dollars" was imposed on "any person who shall employ such Negro or Mulatto, or otherwise encourage him to remain in the State," with the added stipulation that "all contracts made with any Negro or Mulatto coming into the State, contrary to the provisions of the foregoing section, shall be void." Those Blacks or Mulattoes already residing in the State at the time of the constitution's adoption were allowed to remain, though funds collected from fines were to be set aside to provide for their colonization.[16] This amendment received the ap-

---

15. Ibid., page 574.

16. Indiana Constitution (1851), Article XIII, Sections 1-3. An interesting case arose a few years later when Arthur Barkshire, a Black man of the town of Rising Sun, brought a Negress named Elizabeth Keith across the border from Ohio and married her in Ohio county on June 18, 1854. He was convicted and fined $10 by the County Common Pleas Court for "encouraging a Negro to remain in the State of Indiana," and upon appeal, the State Supreme Court not only upheld the lower court's ruling, but also invalidated the marriage: "The policy of the state is . . . clearly evolved. It is to exclude any further ingress of negroes, and to remove those already among us as speedily as possible. A constitutional policy so clearly conducive to the separation and ultimate good of both races should be rigidly enforced" (*Barkshire vs. Indiana* [1856], 7 Ind. 389).

proval of a 90,000 majority — or five-sixths — of the popular vote.[17]

In his address to the legislature on December 30, 1850, Governor Joseph A. Wright cited the continuing need for such discriminatory laws as a means to encourage free Blacks to avoid Indiana and ultimately to leave the country: "The subject of the colonization of the free blacks is now beginning to receive that attention which its importance demands. The circumstances which surround us, are pressing our people to look into this subject in the right light, and in a proper spirit. . . . We in the north are adopting extraordinary means for removing them, by prohibiting them from holding property, excluding them from the protection of the laws, and denying them any rights whatever."[18] In 1852, the General Assembly formed the Indiana Colonization Board and began providing funds to assist resident free Blacks to emigrate to Liberia. This venture, however, proved to be a failure after only 83 Negroes participated in the program with a mere $65 per person being allocated for their transportation and resettlement.[19]

Things were not much different in Lincoln's own State of Illinois. Anti-Negro legislation began there only one year after the State was organized and admitted to the Union,

---

17. Williams, *Negro Race in America*, Volume II, pages 119-120; Richard F. Nation, "Violence and the Rights of African Americans in Civil War-Era Indiana: The Case of James Hays," *Indiana Magazine of History*, Volume C, Number 3 (September 2004), page 216.

18. *Journal of the House of Representatives of the State of Indiana During the Thirty-Fifth Session of the General Assembly* (Indianapolis, Indiana: J. P. Chapman, 1851), page 39.

19. Mary Anthrop, "Indiana Emigrants to Liberia," *The Indiana Historian*, March 2000, page 9.

the purpose of which was, in the words of the State supreme court, "to prevent the influx of that most unacceptable population."[20] On March 30, 1819, an act went into effect which stated that "no black or mulatto person shall be permitted to settle or reside in this State, unless he or she shall first produce a certificate signed by some judge or some clerk of some court of the United States, of his or her actual freedom." All free Blacks were required by this law to register themselves along with evidence of their freedom in the county where they intended to reside, and it also prohibited the employment of any Negro or Mulatto who had not been so registered. Furthermore, this act prescribed "lashes on his or her bare back" for slaves found "ten miles from the tenement of his or her master" (a maximum of thirty-five lashes), "being on the plantation or in the tenement of another than the master, not being sent on lawful business" (ten lashes), and for the gathering of three or more slaves "for the purpose of dancing or reveling either by day or night" (thirty-nine lashes).[21]

"Before 1840, and several years after, the negro had no legal status in Illinois," wrote one historian. "He was an ostracized individual, existing, by the sufferance of the people of Illinois, without citizenship and without social recognition."[22] According to the 1840 census, there were only 4,065 Blacks residing in Illinois, or less than one percent of

20. *Eells v. The People* (1843), 4 Scammon 513.

21. *The Revised Laws of Illinois* (Vandalia, Illinois: Greiner and Sherman, 1833), page 457.

22. N. Dwight Harris, *History of Negro Servitude in Illinois* (Chicago: A. C. McClurg and Company, 1904), page 226.

the total population.[23] Nevertheless, in the 1847 constitutional convention a resolution was introduced to prohibit further immigration of Blacks into the State. As in the neighboring State of Indiana, this denial of equal rights to free Blacks was intended to encourage their acceptance of colonization as declared by Whig delegate Benjamin Bond of Clinton County: "The only true project . . . by which we can be entirely freed from this nuisance, is by sending the blacks to some other country."[24] James R. Brockman, a Democrat delegate from Brown County, said, "The negroes have no rights in common with the people, they can have no rights; the distinction between the two races is so great as to preclude the possibility of their ever living together upon equal terms."[25] Referring to the "crowds of that race flowing in upon our state, filling up our southern counties with an idle, worthless and degraded population, which not only are a trouble and a nuisance to the communities near which they settle, but also prevent a better population from occupying the lands covered by them," Hezekiah Wead of Fulton County asserted the right of the legislature "to exclude from our soil . . . this negro population, which is emphatically the refuse of humanity," and to "protect the white inhabitants of this state from any further evils and wrongs from this wretched population,

---

23. Jerome B. Meites, "The 1847 Illinois Constitutional Convention and Persons of Color," *Journal of the Illinois State Historical Society*, Volume CVIII, Number 3-4 (Fall/Winter 2015), page 266.

24. Arthur Charles Cole, *The Constitutional Debates of 1847* (Springfield, Illinois: Illinois State Historical Library, 1919), page 202. With the collapse of the Whig party, Bond became a Republican.

25. Cole, ibid., pages 202-203.

which other states are driving out of their limits and forcing into our own."[26]

The resulting State constitution of 1848, which was approved by an overwhelming majority of voters, decreed that representation in the legislature would be determined "according to the number of white inhabitants," restricted suffrage to "white male citizens," and expressly excluded "negroes, mulattoes and Indians" from service in the State militia. It also provided that "the General Assembly shall at its first session under the amended constitution pass such laws as will effectively prohibit free persons of color from immigrating to and settling in this state, and to effectually prevent the owners of slaves from bringing them into this state, for the purpose of setting them free."[27] The General Assembly thereafter adopted a new law in 1853 under which no Negro from another State could remain within Illinois for more than ten days. Beyond that time he was subject to arrest, confinement in jail, and a $50 fine and forcible removal from the State. If unable to pay the fine, the law required the sheriff to auction the offender to any bidder willing to pay the costs and to work him the fewest number of days. If the convicted man did not leave within ten days after completing the required service, the process resumed, but the fine was increased $50 for each additional infraction. Those who would bring into the State "any negro or mulatto slave, whether said slave is set free or not," were subject to a fine of "not less than one hundred dollars, nor more than five hundred dollars," as

---

26. Cole, ibid., pages 862-863.

27. Illinois Constitution (1848), Article III, Section 6; Article VI, Section I; Article VIII, Section 1; Article XIV.

well as "imprison[ment] in the county jail not more than one year. . . ."[28]

The same prohibition of the immigration of Negroes and Mulattoes was again included in the constitution proposed by the convention of 1862.[29] Though the new constitution was rejected by voters, they nevertheless approved by a majority of 100,590 of the separately submitted proposals that prohibited Negro immigration into Illinois and barred their right to vote and hold office.[30] Speaking of this provision, the Republican editor of the *Illinois State Journal* wrote, "The truth is, the nigger is an unpopular institution in the free States. Even those who are unwilling to rob them of all the rights of humanity, and are willing to let them have a spot on earth on which to live and to labor and to enjoy the fruits of their toil, do not care to be brought into close contact with them."[31] So extreme was Illinois considered by Northern Abolitionists that it was sarcastically referred to as "the newest slave state in the Union."[32] "What kind of people are the people of Illinois?"

---

28. *Laws of Illinois*, 18 G.A. Act of February 12, 1853, pages 57-60. This bill had been introduced by John A. Logan, who would later serve as a prominent general in the Union army during the war.

29. Illinois Constitution (proposed 1862), Article XVIII, Section 1. Although this constitution was not approved, the previous prohibition of Negro immigration remained operative until a new constitution was ratified in 1870.

30. David W. Lusk, *Politics and Politicians: A Succinct History of the Politics of Illinois From 1856 to 1884* (Springfield, Illinois: H. W. Rokker, 1887), pages 334-335.

31. "The Nigger in the New Constitution," *Illinois State Journal*, March 22, 1862.

32. William Lloyd Garrison, *The Liberator*, April 1, 1853. Actually, slave-

Frederick Douglass once asked. "Were they born and nursed of women as other people are? Or are they the off-spring of wolves and tigers, and only taught to prey upon all flesh pleasing to their bloody taste? If they are members of the human family, by what spirit are they animated? Is it from heaven or is it from hell?"[33] Even Lincoln's secretaries, John G. Nicolay and John Hay, referred to Illinois' Black laws as "a code of Draconian ferocity" which "visit[ed] the immigration of free negroes with penalties of the most savage description."[34] However, there is no record that Lincoln ever objected to such laws or ever gave his support to those seeking their repeal. It should also be

---

ery continued to exist in Illinois until 1863 even though the Northwest Ordinance required that it be a free State. The State constitution of 1818 stipulated that "slavery and involuntary servitude" could not be "introduced," except as punishment for crime. Thus, those who were already slaves remained, and were bought and sold, as such. The constitution did allow for "indentured servitude," which often lasted decades, and in some cases, up to 99 years — essentially slavery under another name (Theodore Calvin Pease, *The Frontier State, 1818-1848* [Chicago: A. C. McClurg & Company, 1919], page 49). According to the 1810 census, there were 168 slaves in Illinois; in 1820 — two years after it achieved statehood — there were 917, thus making it the only Northern State to have an increase in its slave population (Harris, *Negro Servitude in Illinois*). Four of Illinois' governors were slaveholders: Shadrach Bond (owned 14 slaves), Edward Coles (owned 20), Ninian Edwards (bought and sold "indentured servants"), and John Reynolds (owned seven slaves). According the Servitude and Emancipation Index maintained by the State Archive, the last documented emancipation in Illinois was in St. Clair County in 1863 (online at www.ilsos.gov).

33. "The Black Law of Illinois," *Douglass' Monthly,*, March 18, 1853.

34. John G. Nicolay and John Hay, *Abraham Lincoln: A History* (New York: The Century Company, 1914), Volume I, pages 144-145.

remembered that it was in Alton, Illinois that Abolitionist newspaper editor Elijah Lovejoy was murdered by a mob for operating his press there in 1837.[35]

Many similar laws could be cited from the Northeastern and New England States to prove correct the observation that "prejudice of race appears to be stronger in the States that have abolished slavery, than in those where it still exists. . . ."[36] Even when the laws in some of the older Eastern States appeared more lenient than those of the newer Western States, and a semblance of equal rights was accorded to Negro residents, the pervading public prejudice nevertheless maintained an extra-legal distinction between the races:

> In virtually every phase of existence, Negroes found themselves systematically separated from whites. They were either excluded from railway cars, omnibuses, stagecoaches, and steamboats or assigned to special "Jim Crow" sections; they sat, when permitted, in secluded and remote corners of theaters and lecture halls; they could not enter most hotels, restaurants, and resorts, except as servants; they prayed in "Negro pews" in the white churches, and if partaking of the sacrament of the Lord's Supper, they waited until the whites had been served the bread and wine. Moreover, they were often educated in segregated schools, punished in segregated prisons, nursed in segregated hospi-

35. John M. Krum, "The Death of Elijah P. Lovejoy: A Voice From the Past," *Journal of the Illinois State Historical Society*, Volume IV, January 1, 1912.

36. Alexis de Tocqueville, *Democracy in America* (London: George Allard, 1838), page 338.

tals, and buried in segregated cemeteries. . . . To most northerners, segregation constituted not a departure from democratic principles, as certain foreign critics alleged, but simply the working out of natural laws, the inevitable consequence of the racial inferiority of the Negro. God and Nature had condemned the blacks to perpetual subordination. . . . Integration, it was believed, would result in a disastrous mixing of the races.[37]

Northerners generally did not want their White communities tainted by what they considered "the pestilential presence of the black man,"[38] and due to an abiding dread that emancipation of slaves in the South would send hordes of free Negroes northward, public sentiment was usually opposed, and often violently so, to Abolitionism. One notable incident was the four-day riot in New York City that began on July 7, 1834 when several thousand Whites gathered at the Chatham Street Chapel to break up a scheduled anti-slavery meeting, later targeting the homes, businesses, churches, and other buildings associated with Negroes and their Abolitionist supporters. The main impetus of the riot was the rumor that the Abolitionists were advocating racial intermarriage.[39] On October 21, 1835, William Lloyd Garrison, the fanatical editor of *The Liberator*, was on his way to give a lecture at the Female Anti-Slavery

37. Litwack, *North of Slavery*, pages 97-98.

38. Thomas M. Day, "Sam and Sambo," *The Courant* (Hartford, Connecticut), March 6, 1856.

39. Edwin G. Burrows and Mike Wallace, *Gotham: a History of New York City to 1898* (New York: Oxford University Press, 1998), pages 556-559.

Society in Boston when he was attacked by an anti-Aboli-
tionist mob and dragged through the streets by a rope.
He was rescued by the mayor and spent the night in the
city jail "just in season to save him from a fate he well
deserved, and which no one can contemplate without a
shudder!"[40] Anti-slavery poet John Greenleaf Whittier
and British Abolitionist George Thompson were likewise
stoned by protestors in Concord, New Hampshire when
they stopped there on a speaking tour of the New England States.[41]

Attempts to establish integrated schools, and sometimes even segregated schools for Blacks, in the Northeast
met with exceptional opposition. One notable example was
Prudence Crandall's Female Boarding School in Canterbury, Connecticut which opened for business in 1831,
offering courses in geography, history, grammar, arithme-
tic, reading, and writing. Initially an all-White establishment, Crandall decided to admit one Negro girl after being
introduced to Garrison's *Liberator* newspaper in September,
1832. As a result, all the White students were removed by
their parents and the school was forced to close. With the
support of Garrison, Crandall reopened as the School for
Young Ladies and Little Misses of Color and began receiving Black students from the surrounding areas in Connecticut, as well as Boston, Providence, New York, and Philadelphia. After a town meeting determined her school to be a
public nuisance, Crandall became the target of threats and

40. "The Boston Riot," *Hampshire Gazette* (Northampton, Massachusetts), October 28, 1835.

41. W. Sloane Kennedy, *John Greenleaf Whittier: His Life, Genius, and
Writings* (Boston: D. Lothrop, 1886), pages 122-125.

acts of violence and was eventually arrested in July, 1833 for violating a new law which prohibited schools from teaching Black students from outside the State.[42] The trial was prosecuted in October by Andrew T. Judson, a Congressman from Connecticut and later judge for the Sixth Federal District, who spoke in behalf of the community: ". . . [W]e are not merely opposed to the establishment of that school in Canterbury; we mean there shall not be such a school set up anywhere in our State. The colored people can never rise from their menial condition in our country; they ought not to be permitted to rise here. They are an inferior race of beings, and never call or ought to be recognized as the equals of the whites. Africa is the place for them. I am in favor of the Colonization scheme. Let the niggers and their descendants be sent back to their fatherland. . . ."[43] The case was appealed to the Connecticut supreme court where it was dismissed on a procedural technicality in July, 1834. Not long thereafter, vandals attempted to burn the building and fearing for the safety of herself, her family, and her students, Crandall finally closed the school permanently on Septem-

---

42. This law had been passed by the State legislature at the specific request of the townspeople of Canterbury (John C. Hurd, *The Law of Freedom and Bondage in the United States* [Boston: Little, Brown and Company, 1858], Volume II, pages 45-46).

43. Samuel Joseph May, *Some Recollections of Our Antislavery Conflict* (Boston: Fields, Osgood and Company, 1869), page 48. In late 1839, Judson presided over the *Amistad* civil case, ruling on January 13, 1840 that the Blacks aboard the ship were free Africans and not slaves, and ordered that they should be returned to Africa at the Government's expense. Judson's ruling was upheld on March 9, 1841 by the Supreme Court, with Roger B. Taney presiding as Chief Justice.

ber 10, 1834 and fled to Massachusetts.[44]

A similar situation occurred the following year in the New Hampshire town of Canaan. When the Noyes Academy opened its doors to about forty students — both White and Black — in March, many New England Abolitionists excitedly predicted that the institution would be an example for other academies throughout the region to follow suit. The townspeople had other ideas. After a few months of bitter agitation, a mob assembled at the academy on July 4 with torches, axes, and clubs, but was dispersed by the local magistrate. A town meeting was thereafter convened where the school was declared a nuisance and its closing was determined "in the *interest* of the town, the *honor* of the State, and the *good* of the whole community" (emphasis in original).[45] Among the resolutions passed were the following:

> ... [R]esolved, that we view with abhorrence every attempt to introduce among us a black population, and that we will use all lawful means to counteract such introduction. . . .
>
> Resolved, that we view with abhorrence the attempt of the Abolitionists to establish a school in this town, for the instruction of the sable sons and daughters of Africanus, in common with our own sons and daughters and that we view with contempt every white man and woman who may have pledged themselves to receive

---

44. Prudence's brother, Reuben, was arrested in Washington, D.C. on August 10, 1835 for possession of Abolitionist material with intent to distribute. During his eight-month incarceration, he contracted tuberculosis from which he died in 1836 at the age of 30.

45. Litwack, *North of Slavery*, page 119.

black boarders or to compel their own children to associate with them.

Resolved, that we will not send our children to any
Academy or High school, where black children are
educated in common with white children, nor in any way
knowingly encourage such schools.

On August 10, several hundred men from Canaan and
neighboring towns arrived at the school with 95 yoke of
oxen and pulled the building from its foundation, dragging
it a mile down the road. A cannon was fired at the houses
where students were boarding and a spokesman for the mob
triumphantly announced that "the abolitionist monster that
ascended out of the bottomless pit, is sent headlong to
perdition, and the mourners go about the streets." The
remaining teachers and students of the academy were given
one month to leave the town. When an attempt was made
to rebuild the school three years later, the building was
burned to the ground.[46]

Segregated schools could even be found in the progres-
sive Commonwealth of Massachusetts. When several Blacks
petitioned the Primary School Committee of Boston in 1846
to integrate the city schools, a 38-page report was issued
which argued for continued segregation on the grounds that
Negroes were distinct from the White race "not only . . . in
respect to color, hair, and general physiognomy, but pos-
sessing physical, mental, and moral peculiarities, which
render a promiscuous intermingling in the public schools
disadvantageous, both to them and to the whites. . . ." The

_____

46. William Allen Wallace, *The History of Canaan, New Hampshire* (Concord, New Hampshire: The Rumford Press, 1910), Chapter 18.

committee concluded that "the less the colored and white people become intermingled, the better it will be for both races. . . . We maintain, that the true interest of both races require, that they should be kept distinct."[47] In the neighboring State of New York it was said regarding the Negro's equal access to an education, "To what end are these poor creatures taught knowledge, from the exercise of which they are destined to be debarred? It is surely but a cruel mockery to cultivate talents, when in the present state of public feeling, there is no field open for their useful employment. Be his acquirements what they may, a Negro is still a Negro, or, in other words, a creature marked out for degradation, and exclusion from those objects which stimulate the hopes and powers of other men."[48]

Oddly enough, even many Abolitionists themselves held mild to severe segregationist views as well as a belief in the innate inferiority of the Black man. It was not uncommon for them to object to the inclusion of Negroes in their anti-slavery societies. For example, the famous Unitarian theologian, William Ellery Channing of Boston, said, "[W]e ought never to have permitted our colored brethren to unite with us in our associations."[49] When Blacks were invited to join the Female Anti-Slavery Society of Fall River,

---

47. *Report to the Primary School Committee, June 15, 1846, on the Petition of Sundry Colored Persons, for the Abolition of the Schools for Colored Children, With the City Solicitor's Opinion* (Boston: J. H. Eastburn, 1846), pages 7-8, 13.

48. Thomas Hamilton, *Men and Manners in America* (Edinburgh, Scotland: William Blackwood, 1833), Volume I, page 92..

49. Charles H. Wesley, "The Negro's Struggle For Freedom in its Birthplace," *Journal of Negro History*, Volume XXX (1945), page 74.

Massachusetts, it "raised such a storm among some of the leading members that for a time, it threatened the dissolution of the Society" because it would not be tolerated "thus putting them on an equality with ourselves."[50] Accompanying these views were often disparaging remarks about the Negroes' appearance and behavior. William Lloyd Garrison wrote, "The black color of the body, the wooly hair, the thick lips, and other peculiarities of the African forms so striking a contrast to the Caucasian race, that they may be distinguished at a glance. . . . They are branded by the hand of nature with a perpetual mark of disgrace."[51] Hinton Rowan Helper, the author of the infamous 1857 Abolitionist book, *The Impending Crisis of the South*,[52] described the Black

---

50. Elizabeth Buffum Chace and Lucy Buffum Lovell, *Two Quaker Sisters* (New York, Liveright Publishing Corporation, 1937), pages 119-120.

51. *The Liberator*, January 22, 1831.

52. Hinton Rowan Helper, *The Impending Crisis of the South: How To Meet It* (New York: A.B. Burdick, Publishers, 1857). Helper, a native of North Carolina who had relocated to New York, wrote, "It is against slavery on the whole, and against slaveholders as a body, that we wage an exterminating war," referring to slaveholders as "more criminal than common murderers," and suggesting that they would "become the victims of white non-slaveholding vengeance by day, and of barbarous massacre by the negroes at night" (pages 129, 147). William Seward declared *The Impending Crisis* to be "a work of great merit; rich, yet accurate in statistical information, and logical in analogies," and predicted that "it will exert a great influence on the public mind, in favor of truth and justice" (letter of endorsement, June 28, 1857; Stephen D. Carpenter, *The Logic of History: Five Hundred Political Texts Being Concentrated Extracts of Abolitionism* [Madison, Wisconsin: self-published, 1864], page 63). The Republicans in Congress also paid for the free circulation of one hundred thousand copies of a later abridged edition of this book throughout the Northern States in 1858

man as "a very different and inferior creature" who is "by nature, of an exceedingly low and grovelling disposition." He viewed the White man as the "predestined supplanter of the black races," and he openly denounced the radical agenda of "forced political, religious, civil, and social equality of the white and black races" as a "most foul and wicked thing."[53]

According to the *Chicago Tribune*, "The doctrine of the Abolition party is, to let the African race alone, neither marry nor cohabit with them; to give them their freedom; treat them as human beings; pay them for their work; separate the whites from adulterous communication with them, and preserve the purity of the Caucasian blood from African admixture."[54] Horace Greeley, Republican editor of the *New York Tribune*, said that "we make no pretensions to special interest in or liking for the African Race. . . . [W]e maintain the right of every man to himself and his own limbs and muscles . . . but we do not like negroes, and heartily wish no individual of that race had ever been brought to America. We hope the day will come when the whole negro race in this country, being fully at liberty, will gradually, peacefully, freely draw off and form a community by themselves somewhere near the Equator, or join their brethren in lineage in Africa or

---

(Rushmore G. Horton, *A Youth's History of the Great Civil War of the United States From 1861 to 1865* [New York: Van Evrie, Horton and Company, 1868], page 59).

53. Hinton Rowan Helper, *Black Negroes in Negroland* (New York: Carleton, 1868), pages viii-ix. Helper was appointed by Abraham Lincoln as United States Consul to Buenos Aires in November of 1861.

54. *Chicago Tribune*, March 14, 1863.

the West Indies."[55] On another occasion, he declared that, "nine-tenths of the free blacks have no idea of settling themselves to work, except as the hirelings and servitors of white men; no idea of building a church or other serious enterprise, except through beggary of the whites. As a class, the blacks are indolent, improvident, servile and licentious; and their inveterate habit of appealing to white benevolence, or compassion whenever they realize a want or encounter a difficulty, is eminently baneful and enervating."[56] He also admitted that, "in their private conversation, no men are more frank in acknowledgment and reproof of negro sloth and vice than Abolitionists."[57] Theodore Parker of Boston noted, "There are inferior races which have always borne the same ignoble relation to the rest of men, and *always will*. . . . [I]n twenty generations, the negroes will stand just where they are now; that is, if they have not disappeared" (emphasis in original).[58] Furthermore, "the Anglo-Saxon with common sense does not like the Africanization of America; he wishes the superior race to multiply, rather than the inferior."[59] Even more to the point,

---

55. *New York Tribune*, February 29, 1860.

56. Ibid., September 22, 1855.

57. Ibid., August 3, 1857

58. Letter to Miss Hunt, November 16, 1857; Octavius Brooks Frothingham, *Theodore Parker: A Biography* (Boston: Osgood, 1874), page 467. Parker had been one of the Secret Six who financed John Brown in his failed mission to create a slave uprising throughout the South.

59. Theodore Parker, *John Brown's Expedition Reviewed in a Letter from Rev. Theodore Parker, at Rome, to Francis Jackson, Boston* (Boston: The Fraternity, 1860), page 14.

was Ralph Waldo Emerson's observation: "The abolitionist wishes to abolish slavery, but because he wishes to abolish the black man."[60] Many other examples could be given to demonstrate that, in many cases, Blacks were viewed even by their professed friends in the anti-slavery movement as occupying "a mere secondary, underling position . . . and any thing more than this, is not a matter of course . . . but . . . by mere sufferance."[61]

60. Ralph H. Orth and Alfred R. Ferguson (editor), *The Journals and Miscellaneous Notebooks of Ralph Waldo Emerson* (Cambridge: Harvard University Press, 1977), Volume XIII, page 198.

61. Martin Robinson Delany, *The Condition, Elevation, Emigration, and Destiny of the Colored People of the United States* (Philadelphia: self-published, 1852), page 27.

CHAPTER FOUR

The Rise of the Republican Party

Northerners' aversion to Blacks applied not only to their communities and States, but also to the western Territories from which new States would be derived. In fact, the Free Soil party was formed in Buffalo, New York in 1848 for the express purpose of confining Negroes to the Southern States and preventing their immigration, whether as slaves or as freemen, into the Territories. In other words, "The cry of Free Men was raised, not for the extension of liberty to the black man, but for the protection of the liberty of the white."[1] The words of the Free Soil leaders themselves justified this assessment. In a speech delivered in Albany, New York on October 29, 1847, David Wilmot of Pennsylvania, a foremost member of the party and author of the celebrated Wilmot Proviso,[2] said:

---

1. Frederick Douglass, *The North Star*, Rochester, New York, January 12, 1849.

2. The Wilmot Proviso was a rider attached to an appropriations bill during the Mexican War that attempted to ban slavery from any Territory acquired as a result of the war. It was approved by the Northern-

An effort is made to bring odium upon this movement [Free Soilism], as one designed especially for the
benefit of the black race. While its success would ensure
the redemption, at an earlier day, of the negro from his
bondage and his chains, I deny that it was especially for
him that the Proviso was offered; or that he is the party
most deeply interested in its result. It has, with justice
and propriety, been called the "White Man's Proviso"
and the Free White Laborer has by far the deepest stake
in its failure or success. For him it solves the momen-
tous question, whether that vast country, between the
Rio Grande and the Pacific, shall be given up to the servile labor of the black, or be preserved for the free labor
of the white man. Shall that fair clime, with its rich soil
and abundant resources, capable of sustaining a population of fifty millions of freemen, be preserved for the
white man and his posterity, or shall it be given up to
the African and his descendants? This is the great ulti-
mate question involved in the present struggle between
Freedom and Slavery. . . . In God's name, as we love our
country and our race, let us stop in this mad career of
human slavery. The negro race already occupy enough
of this fair continent. Let us keep what remains for ourselves, and our children. . . .³

Addressing Congress that same year, Wilmot denied
any intention to interfere with Southern institutions, stat-
ing that he had "no squeamish sensitiveness upon the sub-

---

dominated House of Representatives, but failed in the Senate where
the sections were still evenly balanced.

3. *Herkimer Convention, The Voice of New York: Proceedings of the
Herkimer Mass Convention of Oct. 26, 1847* (*Albany Atlas* Extra, November 1847), page 14.

ject of slavery, no morbid sympathy for the slave." Instead, his concern was to "plead the cause and the rights of white freemen" and to "preserve to free white labor a fair country, a rich inheritance, where the sons of toil, of my own race and own color, can live without the disgrace which association with negro slavery brings upon free labor."[4]

William Seward, an anti-slavery New York Whig and supporter of the Free Soil party who would later serve in Lincoln's cabinet as Secretary of State, likewise declared in the Senate on March 11, 1850, "The population of the United States consists of natives of Caucasian origin, and exotics of the same derivation. The native mass readily assimilates to itself and absorbs the exotic, and these constitute one homogenous people. The African race, bond and free, and the aborigines, savage and civilised, being incapable of such assimilation and absorption, remain distinct, and, owing to their peculiar condition, constitute inferior masses, and may be regarded as accidental if not disturbing political forces."[5] As late as September 4, 1860, Seward's views had not changed:

> How natural has it been to assume that the motive of those who have protested against the extension of slavery, was an unnatural sympathy with the negro instead of what it always has really been, concern for the welfare of the white man. . . .
>
> The great fact is now fully realized that the African race here is a foreign and feeble element, like the Indians, incapable of assimilation, . . . and that it is a pitiful

---

4. *Congressional Globe*, Twenty-Ninth Congress, Second Session, February 1847, Appendix, page 317.

5. Ibid., Thirty-First Congress, First Session, Appendix, page 261.

exotic, unwisely and unnecessarily transplanted into
our fields, and which it is unprofitable to cultivate at the
cost of the desolation of the native vineyard.[6]

The Republican party came into existence in 1854 as
the Whig party was dying out, and it absorbed the rem-
nants of the equally moribund Liberty, Free Soil, and
American ("Know Nothing") parties. Though often
claimed to be the party that "freed the slaves" and "cham-
pioned Black civil rights" over against the "White supremacy" of the Democrats,[7] there was no substantial difference
in how most Republicans viewed the Black man. In fact,
according to one source, a poll of the Republicans in the
Northwestern States would "not find one in every thousand who is in favor of extending equal social and political
privileges to the negroes."[8] For example, Senator John
Sherman of Ohio, brother of famed Union General William
T. Sherman said, "In the State where I live, we do not like
negroes. We do not disguise our dislike. As my friend from

6. William H. Seward, *Speeches of William H. Seward: Lincoln Campaign
1860* (Albany, New York: Weed, Parsons and Company, 1860), pages
5, 6.

7. Such is the argument advanced by former Vanderbilt Professor of
Political Science, Carol Swain, in her Prager University video entitled,
"The Inconvenient Truth About the Republican Party." The video has
been viewed over eight million times since it was posted on the Prager
University website (www.prageru.com) on January 15, 2018. Swain
repeated essentially the same arguments in two other videos: "Civil
Rights and Slavery — Republican and Democrat Parties," and "The
Inconvenient Truth About the Democrat Party."

8. Benjamin Stanton, speech in the House of Representatives, May 3,
1860; *Congressional Globe*, Thirty-Sixth Congress, First Session, page
1910.

Indiana (Mr. Wright) said yesterday: 'The whole people of the Northwestern States are opposed to having many negroes among them and that principle or prejudice has been engraved in the legislation of nearly all of the Northwestern States.'"[9] According to Senator Benjamin F. Wade, also of Ohio, the solution to the "Negro problem" was not only the abolition of slavery, but the removal of the race entirely from the country: ". . . [It has been] said that we Black Republicans were advocates of negro equality, and that we wanted to build up a black government. Sir, it will be one of the most blessed ideas of the times, if it shall come to this, that we will make inducements to every free black among us to find his home in a more congenial climate in Central America or Lower Mexico, and we will be divested of every one of them. . . ."[10]

Lincoln's friend and fellow Illinoisan, Senator Lyman Trumbull, was even more to the point:

> I, for one, am very much disposed to favor the colonization of such free negroes as are willing to go in Cen-

9. *Congressional Globe,* Thirty-Seventh Congress, Second Session, April 2, 1862, page 1491. Sherman here approvingly referred to the speech Senator Joseph A. Wright of Indiana made the previous day in the Senate in which he said, ". . . [W]e do not intend to allow our region of the country to be overrun with the black race. Such is the prejudice, such is the settled conviction of our people, that the wall which we have erected is to stand. We intend to have in our State as far as possible, a white population, and we do not intend to have our jails and penitentiaries filled with the free blacks" (ibid., page 1468). Though a Democrat, Wright supported the Union invasion of the South.

10. Ibid., Thirty-Sixth Congress, Second Session, December 17, 1860, page 104. It should be noticed that the date of Wade's speech preceded the secession of South Carolina by a mere three days.

tral America. I want to have nothing to do either with the free negro or the slave negro. We, the Republican party, are the white man's party. We are for free white men, and for making white labor respectable and honorable, which it never can be when negro slave labor is brought into competition with it. We wish to settle the Territories with free white men, and we are willing that this negro race should go anywhere that it can to better its condition, wishing them God speed wherever they go. We believe it is better for us that they should not be among us. I believe it will be better for them to go elsewhere.[11]

Gideon Welles of Connecticut, later to serve in Lincoln's Cabinet as Secretary of the Navy, was even more to the point: "It is not the cause of the negro, but that of the . . . white man that is involved in this question" of the Territories.[12]

It is important to keep in mind that the Republican party was not a monolithic organization but rather a loose coalition of otherwise disparate factions seeking a common goal: the permanent reduction of Southern influence in the Union and the concentration of power in Washington. Even

---

11. *Speech of Hon. Lyman Trumbull, of Illinois, at a Mass Meeting in Chicago, August 7, 1858* (Washington, D.C.: Buell and Blanchard, Printers, 1858), page 13. In addition to being published in pamphlet form, Trumbull's speech was also printed in several leading Republican newspapers and received a lot of praise. Lincoln supported Trumbull's reelection to the Senate in 1860, calling him "peculiar for his rigid honesty, his hightoned independence & his unswerving devotion to principle" (Michael Burlingame, *Abraham Lincoln: A Life* [Baltimore: Johns Hopkins University Press, 2008], Volume I, page 403).

12. Matthew Warshauer, *Connecticut in the American Civil War: Slavery, Sacrifice, and Survival* (Middleton, Connecticut: Wesleyan University Press, 2011), page 39.

though the Northern Abolitionists aligned themselves with the Republicans, the party's official stance on slavery was not opposition to its continuance in any of the States where it already existed, but only to its extension into the Territories. Such was clearly stated at the Chicago Convention of May 16-18, 1860, the second plank of whose platform declared, "That the maintenance inviolate of the rights of the states, and especially the right of each state to order and control its own domestic institutions according to its own judgment exclusively, is essential to that balance of powers on which the perfection and endurance of our political fabric depends. . . ."[13] However, as we have seen, opposition to the extension of slavery was more about keeping the Territories free of Negroes than any pretended humanitarianism on the part of leading Republicans. Not only were the Territories viewed as the future home for White laborers only, but it was also feared that should slavery be allowed to expand into the new lands, free Blacks would follow in large numbers, thereby endangering the racial purity of the settlers. Lincoln had expressed this attitude at Springfield, Illinois on June 26, 1857: "There is a natural disgust in the minds of nearly all white people, to the idea of an indiscriminate amalgamation of the white and black races. . . . A separation of the races is the only perfect preventive of amalgamation; but as immediate separation is impossible, the next best thing is to keep them apart where they are not already together. If white and black people never get together in Kansas, they will never

13. George O. Seilhamer, *History of the Republican Party: Narrative and Critical History, 1856-1898* (New York: Judge Publishing Company, 1899), Volume I, page 81.

mix blood in Kansas"[14] — thus creating what was called a race of "mixed breed bastards."[15] So well known were these facts at the time that some of the more radical Abolitionists, such as William Lloyd Garrison, complained bitterly that the Republicans were "a complexional party, exclusively for white men, not for all men, white or black."[16] Frederick Douglass also observed, "The Democrats have declared themselves our enemies, and the Republicans have not declared themselves our friends. While Democrats would admit the black man into Kansas as a slave, Republicans would seem to wish to exclude him as a free man. . . . One party would enslave him, and the other party would drive him from the face of all the earth over which they have power."[17]

---

14. Basler, *Collected Works of Lincoln*, Volume II, pages 405, 408.

15. According to Abolitionist Methodist minister James Mitchell of Indiana, "Our republican system was meant for a homogeneous people. As long as the Negroes continue to live with the whites they will constitute a threat to the national life. Family life might also collapse and the increase of 'the mixed breed bastards,' might some day challenge the supremacy of the white man" (statement to Lincoln on May 15, 1862; Roy P. Basler [editor], *Abraham Lincoln Quarterly* [Springfield, Illinois: Abraham Lincoln Association, 1950], Volume VI, Number 3, page 172). On August 4, 1862, Mitchell was appointed by Lincoln as Commissioner of Negro Emigration in connection with the latter's proposed South American colonization plan. He also organized the President's meeting with the Black delegation at the White House on August 14 (Benjamin Quarles, *Lincoln and the Negro*, pages 115–116).

16. James A. Rawley, *Race and Politics: "Bleeding Kansas" and the Coming of the Civil War* (Lincoln, Nebraska: University of Nebraska Press, 1979), page 151.

17. Patrick Rael, *Eighty-Eight Years: The Long Death of Slavery in the United States, 1777-1865* (Athens, Georgia: University of Georgia Press, 2015), page 212.

CHAPTER FIVE

The War Was Not Fought Over Slavery

From his nomination and election to his final days in the White House, Lincoln never deviated from his party's platform in his approach to the subject of slavery. In a December 15, 1860 letter to John A. Gilmer, a Congressman from North Carolina, he complained that his political foes were accusing him of "shift[ing] the ground upon which [he had] been elected," intending to use the executive office to effect an abolition of slavery in the capital and also to interfere with the institution in the South: "Carefully read . . . the volume of Joint Debates between Senator Douglas and myself, with the Republican Platform adopted at Chicago, and all your questions will be substantially answered. I have no thought of recommending the abolition of slavery in the District of Columbia, nor the slave trade among the slave states, even on the conditions indicated; and if I were to make such recommendation, it is quite clear Congress would not follow it." Lincoln concluded his letter with the recommendation of the repeal of any laws in Illinois and other Northern States that were "in conflict with the fugitive slave clause, or any other part of the constitution."[1] On December 22, he wrote a similar letter to soon-to-be Confederate Vice President Alexander H. Stephens of Georgia:

> Do the people of the South really entertain fears that a Republican administration would, directly, or indirectly, interfere with their slaves, or with them, about their slaves? If they do, I wish to assure you . . . that there is no cause for such fears. The South would be in no more danger in this respect, than it was in the days of Washington. . . .
>
> You think slavery is right and ought to be extended; while we think it is wrong and ought to be restricted. That I suppose is the rub. It certainly is the only substantial difference between us.[2]

Just a few months later, Lincoln repeated this same sentiment in his first Inaugural Address on March 4, 1861:

> Apprehension seems to exist among the people of the Southern States that by the accession of a Republican Administration their property and their peace and personal security are to be endangered. There has never been any reasonable cause for such apprehension. Indeed, the most ample evidence to the contrary has all the while existed and been open to their inspection. It is found in nearly all the published speeches of him who now addresses you. I do but quote from one of those speeches when I declare that — I have no purpose, directly or indirectly, to interfere with the institution of

---

1. Basler, *Collected Works of Lincoln*, Volume IV, page 152.

2. Basler, ibid., page 160.

slavery in the States where it exists. I believe I have no lawful right to do so, and I have no inclination to do so. Those who nominated and elected me did so with full knowledge that I had made this and many similar declarations and had never recanted them. . . .

I now reiterate these sentiments, and in doing so I only press upon the public attention the most conclusive evidence of which the case is susceptible that the property, peace, and security of no section are to be in any wise endangered by the now incoming Administration.[3]

Under Lincoln's direction, Secretary of State Seward made the following statement in a diplomatic circular intended for the courts of Europe:

The condition of slavery in the several States will remain just the same. . . . The rights of the States, and the condition of every human being in them, will remain subject to exactly the same laws and form of administration, whether the revolution shall succeed or whether it shall fail. Their constitutions and laws and customs, habits and institutions in either case will remain the same. It is hardly necessary to add to this incontestable statement the further fact that the new President, as well as the citizens through whose suffrages he has come into the administration, has always repudiated all designs whatever, and wherever imputed to him and them, of disturbing the system of slav-

3. James D. Richardson, *A Compilation of the Messages and Papers of the Presidents* (Washington D. C.: Bureau of National Literature, 1897), Volume V, page 3206.

ery as it is existing under the Constitution and laws.[4]

For his consistent unwillingness to deviate from this policy Lincoln was heavily criticized by the Northern Abolitionists,[5] who saw in the war an opportunity to deal a death blow to the South's "peculiar institution." Martin F. Conway of Kansas complained thusly of the "save the Union" policy in the House of Representatives: "I cannot see that the policy of the Administration . . . tends, in the smallest degree, to an anti-slavery result. The principle governing it is, that the constitutional Union, as it existed prior to the rebellion, remains intact; that the local laws, usages, and institutions of the seceded States are to be sedulously respected. . . . There is not . . . the most distant intimation of giving actual freedom to the slave in any event. . . ."[6] Thaddeus Stevens of Pennsylvania likewise stated in the House, "Sir, I can no longer agree that this Administration is pursuing a wise policy. . . . Its policy ought to be to order our army, wherever they go, to free the slaves, to enlist them, to arm them, to discipline them as they have been enlisted, armed and disciplined everywhere else, and as they can be here, and set them shooting their masters, if they will not submit to this Government."[7]

---

4. Letter to United States Ambassador to France, William L. Dayton, April 22, 1861; *Papers Relating to Foreign Affairs* (Washington, D.C.: Government Printing Office, 1861), Volume I, page 198.

5. T. Harry Williams, *Lincoln and the Radicals* (Madison, Wisconsin: The University of Wisconsin Press, 1941).

6. *Congressional Globe*, Thirty-Seventh Congress, First Session, December 12, 1862, page 83.

7. Ibid., Second Session, July 5, 1862, page 3127.

Lincoln especially incurred the displeasure of his detractors when, during the first year of the war, he revoked the emancipation edicts of two of his generals in the field and returned the Negroes to their masters. The first incident occurred in the fall of 1861, when Major-General John C. Frémont,[8] commanding the Department of the West from Saint Louis, issued a proclamation on August 30, placing the State of Missouri under martial law and confiscating the property of those bearing arms against the United States, thereby declaring freedom to their slaves.[9] The Abolitionists were ecstatic and lauded Frémont as a hero: "From that moment, Fremont became more than a general – to millions, especially in New England and among the German and Yankee of the West, he became a symbol. His name represented the crusade for the extinction of slavery."[10] However, while the radicals rejoiced over the decree as "welcome manna from heaven,"[11] many others had the opposite reaction. The outcry among conservatives in the Border States against the "abominable, atrocious, and infamous usurpation"[12] and their demand for Frémont's removal from command was immediate. Lin-

---

8. Frémont had been the 1856 Republican candidate for President and was a favorite with the radical faction of the party.

9. *Official Records of the War of the Rebellion* (Washington, D.C.: Government Printing Office, 1894), Series II, Volume I, page 221.

10. Allan Nevins, *Frémont: Pathmarker of the West* (Lincoln, Nebraska: University of Nebraska Press, 1992), page 503.

11. Williams, *Lincoln and the Radicals*, page 40.

12. Louisville *Courier*; Frank Moore (editor), *The Rebellion Record: A Diary of American Events* (New York: G.P. Putnam, 1864), Volume III, page 34.

coln's close friend, Joshua Speed, sent him an urgent warning: "So fixed is public sentiment in this state against freeing Negroes . . . that you had as well attack the freedom of worship in the North or the right of a parent to teach his child to read as to wage war in the states on such principles."[13] True to Speed's prediction, one Kentucky company of Unionists promptly threw down their weapons and disbanded upon hearing of the edict.[14]

Fearing that the proclamation would ultimately drive Kentucky, as well as Missouri and Maryland, into the arms of the Southern Confederacy,[15] Lincoln sent Frémont a pointed request on September 2 to revoke the order,[16] on the grounds that it was "purely political, and not within the range of military law, or necessity."[17] Frémont refused to comply with the request[18] and sent his wife to Washington to argue for the validity of his proclamation, to which Lincoln responded: "The General should never have dragged the negro into the war. It is a war for a great national object and the negro has nothing to do with it."[19] He

---

13. Letter to Lincoln, September 3, 1861; Lowell H. Harrison, *Lincoln of Kentucky* (Lexington, Kentucky: University Press of Kentucky, 2000), page 225.

14. Benjamin P. Thomas, *Abraham Lincoln: A Biography* (New York: Alfred A. Knopf, 1952), page 275.

15. Letter to Orville H. Browning, September 22, 1861; Basler, *Collected Works of Lincoln*, Volume IV, page 532.

16. *Official Records*, Series II, Volume I, page 766.

17. Basler, *Collected Works of Lincoln*, Volume IV, page 531.

18. *Official Records*, Series I, Volume III, pages 477-478.

19. Pamela Herr and Mary Lee Spence (editors), *Letters of Jessie Benton Frémont* (Chicago: University of Illinois Press, 1993), pages 264-267.

personally revoked Frémont's emancipation edict on September 11,[20] and then removed him on October 24.[21] The erstwhile joy of the Abolitionists turned to wrath, and Lincoln was denounced as "poor white trash,"[22] and other furious epithets, and condemned for "conciliating the contemptible state of Kentucky" while wasting time and resources "to secure the niggers of traitors."[23] In the words of one Negro journalist, his action "hurls back into the hell of slavery the thousands in Missouri rightfully set free by the proclamation of Gen. Fremont, which deprives the cause of the Union of its chiefest hold upon the heart of the public, and which gives to the rebels 'aid and comfort' greater than they could have gained from any other earthly source."[24]

On May 9, 1862, Major General David Hunter, commander of the Department of the South, issued Order 11 from Hilton Head, South Carolina declaring the slaves in South Carolina, Georgia, and Florida "forever free," and ordering the arming of all able-bodied Negroes in those

20. *Official Records*, Series II, Volume I, page 768.

21. Ibid., Series I, Volume III, page 553.

22. Benjamin F. Wade, letter to Zachariah Chandler, September 23, 1861; Williams, *Lincoln and the Radicals*, page 41.

23. George Hoadley, letter to Salmon P. Chase, September 18, 1861; James Ford Rhodes, *History of the United States from the Compromise of 1850: 1860-1862* (New York: The Macmillan Company, 1904), Volume III, page 473. Hoadley sat on the Ohio Superior Court and later became Governor of the State.

24. Robert Hamilton, *Anglo-African*, September 21, 1861; James M. McPherson, *The Negro's Civil War: How American Blacks Felt and Acted During the War For the Union* (New York: Vintage Civil War Library, 2003), page 42.

States.[25] Lincoln first learned of the proclamation in a Northern newspaper and promptly voided the order just as he had done with Frémont's, again voicing his concern that such an action would push slave-holding Unionists to support the Confederacy:

> Whereas there appears in the public prints what purports to be a proclamation of Major General Hunter . . . and whereas, the same is producing some excitement and misunderstanding,
>
> Therefore I, Abraham Lincoln, President of the United States, proclaim and declare that the Government of the United States had no knowledge, information or belief of an intention on the part of General Hunter to issue such a proclamation nor has it yet any authentic information that document is genuine. And further that neither General Hunter nor any other commander or person has been authorized by the Government of the United States to make proclamations declaring the slaves of any State free; and that the supposed proclamation now in question, whether genuine or false, is altogether void so far as respects such declaration.
>
> I further make known that whether it be competent for me as Commander-in-Chief of the Army and Navy to declare the slaves of any State or States free, and whether at any time in any case it shall have become a necessity indispensable to the maintenance of the Government to exercise such supposed power are questions which under my responsibility I reserve to myself and which I cannot feel justified in leaving to the decision of

---

25. *Official Records*, Series II, Volume I, page 818.

commanders in the field.[26]

Again, Lincoln was excoriated by the radicals for his apparent lack of support for the Abolitionist cause. Writing of the above cancellation proclamation, Joseph Medill, editor of the *Chicago Tribune*, opined that "a more injudicious and unjust edict has not been issued since the war began."[27] William Lloyd Garrison predicted that the proclamation "will serve to increase the disgust and uneasiness felt in Europe at our shilly-shallying course, to abate the enthusiasm of the army and friends of freedom universally, and to inspire the rebels with fresh courage and determination."[28] The Abolitionist press and clergy denounced Lincoln's "Pro-slavery Proclamation"[29] as a "disgrace to himself and to the government" and a "crime against humanity and God,"[30] and labelled him as "the man who re-enslaved nearly a million human beings."[31] In his "Prayer

26. Ibid.

27. Letter to Salmon P. Chase, May 30, 1862; John Niven (editor), *The Salmon P. Chase Papers* (Kent, Ohio: Kent State University Press, 1993), Volume III, page 207.

28. Letter to Charles B. Sedgwick, May 20, 1862; Walter M. Merrill (editor), *The Letters of William Lloyd Garrison* (Cambridge: Harvard University Press, 1981), Volume V, page 93.

29. *Pacific Appeal*, June 14, 1862; C. Peter Ripley (editor), *The Black Abolitionist Papers* (Chapel Hill, North Carolina: University of North Carolina Press, 1992), Volume V, page 143.

30. Samuel J. May, Jr., to Richard Webb, May 27, 1862, May Papers, Boston Public Library.

31. Victor B. Howard, *Religion and the Radical Republican Movement, 1860-1870* (Lexington, Kentucky: University Press of Kentucky, 1986), page 28.

of Twenty Millions" open letter to Lincoln, Horace Greeley informed him that "a great portion of those who triumphed in your election . . . are sorely disappointed and deeply pained by the policy you seem to be pursuing with regard to the slaves of Rebels,"and demanded that he stop listening to "certain fossil politicians hailing from the Border Slave States."[32] Lincoln, however, was unmoved by such criticisms. Obviously, if anyone was going to "drag the negro into the war," he was going to do it himself — which he did just four months later, albeit for reasons quite different than is often assumed.

_____

32. *New York Tribune*, August 19, 1862; Moore, *Rebellion Record*, Supplement, Volume I, page 480.

CHAPTER SIX

Lincoln Did Not Free the Slaves

In his monumental work, *The Rise and Fall of the Confederate Government*, former C. S. President, Jefferson Davis, wrote, "The truth remains intact and incontrovertible, that the existence of African servitude was in no wise the cause of the conflict, but only an incident. In the later controversies that arose, however, its effect in operating as a lever upon the passions, prejudices, or sympathies of mankind, was so potent that it has been spread, like a thick cloud, over the whole horizon of historic truth."[1] Davis' assertion was corroborated, not only by the historical facts, but also by the testimony of some very prominent Northern leaders. On May 13, 1861, William T. Sherman, who was at that time in Saint Louis, gave the following observation about the real issue behind the war: "No one now talks of the negro. The integrity of the Union and the relative power of state and general government are the issues in this war. Were it not for the physical geography of the

---

1. Jefferson Davis, *The Rise and Fall of the Confederate Government* (New York: D. Appleton and Company, 1881), Volume I, page 80.

country it might be that the people could consent to divide and separate in peace. But the Mississippi is too grand an element to be divided, and all its extent must of necessity be under one government."[2] Less than three weeks earlier, he had written to his brother in Washington, "On the necessity of maintaining a government and that government the old constitutional one, I have never wavered, but I do recoil from a war, when the negro is the only question."[3] Ulysses S. Grant was also reported to have expressed a similar opinion while still a colonel of the 21st Illinois Infantry.[4]

Despite the claims of modern history revisionists, the core issue of the so-called "Civil War" was not slavery, but

---

2. Walter L. Fleming (editor), *General W. T. Sherman as College President: A Collection of Letters, Documents, and Other Material Chiefly From Private Sources, Relating to the Life and Activities of General William Tecumseh Sherman* (Cleveland, Ohio: The Arthur H. Clark Company, 1912), page 383.

3. Letter to John Sherman, April 25, 1861; ibid., page 381.

4. "I have no doubt in the world that the sole object [of the war] is the restoration of the Union. I will say further, though, that I am a Democrat – every man in my regiment is a Democrat – and whenever I shall be convinced that this war has for its object anything else than what I have mentioned, or that the Government designs using its soldiers to execute the purposes of the abolitionists, I pledge you my honor as a man and a soldier that I will not only resign my commission, but will carry my sword to the other side, and cast my lot with that people" (Matthew Carey, Jr. [pseudonym], *The Democratic Speaker's Hand Book* [Cincinnati, Ohio: Miami Print and Publishing Company, 1868], page 33). Some have disputed the authenticity of this quote, but there is no doubt that Grant did write the following words in 1863: "I never was an Abolitionist, not even what could be called anti-slavery. . . ." (Letter to Henry Wilson, August 30, 1863; Albert Deane Richardson, *A Personal History of Ulysses S. Grant* [Hartford, Connecticut: American Publishing Company, 1868], page 345).

rather a dispute over territorial economics and the relation of the States to the Federal Government.[5] Even Congress itself was clear that the abolition of slavery was not an objective in defeating the "rebellion":

> Resolved, That the present deplorable civil war has been forced upon the country by the disunionists of the Southern States now in revolt against the constitutional Government and in arms around the capital; that in this national emergency Congress, banishing all feeling of mere passion or resentment, will recollect only its duty to the whole country; that this war is not prosecuted upon our part in any spirit of oppression, nor for any purpose of conquest or subjugation, nor purpose of overthrowing or interfering with the rights or established institutions of those States, but to defend and maintain the supremacy of the Constitution and all laws made in pursuance thereof, and to preserve the Union, with all the dignity, equality, and rights of the several States unimpaired; that as soon as these objects are accomplished the war ought to cease.[6]

On the one hand, the vast majority of Southerners had no personal interest in either the continuance or extension of the institution,[7] and on the other, only a small minority

5. This is most evident in South Carolina's December 25, 1860 "Address to the Slaveholding States," in which only two paragraphs out of fourteen are devoted to a discussion of slavery.

6. *Congressional Globe*, Thirty-Seventh Congress, First Session, July 25, 1861, pages 222-223.

7. According to the 1860 census, the White population of the Southern States was 6,184,477, out of which only 347,525 — just under six percent — were slaveholders. Those who owned twenty or more slaves

of radicals in the North desired to transform the war into an Abolitionist crusade. In the summer of 1861, Lincoln told the anti-slavery Presbyterian minister, Charles E. Lester:

> I think [Charles] Sumner and the rest of you [Aboli-tionists] would upset our apple-cart altogether, if you had your way. . . . We didn't go into the war to put *down* Slavery, but to put the flag *back*; and to act differently at this moment, would . . . not only weaken our cause, but smack of bad faith; for I never should have had votes enough to send me here, if the people had supposed I should try to use my power to upset Slavery. Why, the first thing you'd see, would be a mutiny in the army (emphasis in original).[8]

Lincoln not only had to contend with pressure from the

---

were exempted from military service under the Confederate States Conscription Act of 1862. Virginia, the largest of the slave States, was a good sample of the whole. The White population of the Common-wealth in 1860 was fixed at 1,047,299 and the number of slaveholders in that State at only 52,128 (Beverley B. Munford, *Virginia's Attitude Toward Slavery and Secession* [New York: Longmans, Green and Com-pany, 1909], page 125). Of this latter number, "[O]ne-third held but one or two slaves; half held one to four; there were but one hundred and fourteen persons in the whole state who owned as many as a hundred each, and this out of a population of over a million whites" (French Ensor Chadwick, *Causes of the Civil War* [New York: Harper and Brothers Publishers, 1906], page 33). The total number of slaveholders in the Confederate armies was estimated at 200,000, compared with the 350,000 in the Northern army — the total in the latter being over fifty percent higher than in the former (Mildred Lewis Rutherford, *Truths of History* [Athens, Georgia: self-published, 1920], page 14).

8. Charles Edward Lester, *Life and Public Services of Charles Sumner* (New York: United States Publishing Company, 1874), page 359.

Abolitionists within his own party, but also the insinuations of his critics in the Democratic party who had long suspected him of secretly planning to use the war as an excuse to effect a general emancipation of the slaves. Referring to the latter, he said, "My enemies pretend I am now carrying on this war for the sole purpose of abolition. So long as I am President, it shall be carried on for the sole purpose of restoring the Union."[9]

One Abolitionist wrote some years later, "If Mr. Lincoln had been told, when he entered on the Presidency, that before his term of office would expire he would be hailed as 'The Great Emancipator,' he would have treated the statement as equal to one of his own best jokes. Slavery was a thing he did not then want to have disturbed."[10] Nevertheless, in the summer of 1862, Lincoln began working on the draft for what would become the initial Emancipation Proclamation. This document has often been interpreted as evidence that he had evolved in his thoughts on race and was attempting to give a higher humanitarian purpose to the war. However, Lincoln's move was merely strategic and did not involve any substantial change in his policy regarding slavery. On August 22, he had written the following to Horace Greeley:

> I would save the Union. I would save it the shortest way under the Constitution. The sooner the national authority can be restored; the nearer the Union will be

9. Statement to Alexander W. Randall, August 19, 1864; John G. Nicolay and John Hay (editors), *Abraham Lincoln: Complete Works, Comprising His Speeches, Letters, State Papers, and Miscellaneous Writings* (New York: The Century Company, 1894), Volume II, page 562.

10. Hume, *The Abolitionists*, page 143.

"the Union as it was." If there be those who would not save the Union, unless they could at the same time save slavery, I do not agree with them. If there be those who would not save the Union unless they could at the same time destroy slavery, I do not agree with them. My paramount object in this struggle is to save the Union, and is not either to save or destroy slavery. If I could save the Union without freeing any slave I would do it, and if I could save it by freeing all the slaves I would do it; and if I could save it by freeing some and leaving others alone I would do that. What I do in regard to slavery, and the colored race, I do because I believe it helps to save the Union, and what I forbear, I forbear because I do not believe it would help to save the Union.[11]

Along these lines, Lincoln described his proclamation as "a practical war measure, to be decided upon according to the advantages or disadvantages it may offer to the suppression of the rebellion"[12] — a description also found in the document itself. In fact, he based his argument, not on the slaves' humanity, but on the premise that they were property liable to confiscation under the laws of war: "I think the Constitution invests its commander-in-chief with the law of war in time of war. The most that can be said, if so much, is, that the slaves are property. Is there, has there ever been, any question that by the law of war, property, both of enemies and friends, may be taken when needed? And is it not whenever it helps us and hurts the enemy? Armies, the world over, destroy enemies' property when they cannot use it, and even destroy their own to keep it

11. Basler, *Collected Works of Lincoln*, Volume V, page 388.
12. Basler, ibid., page 421.

from the enemy."[13]

A careful examination of the proclamation reveals that it decreed the emancipation only of slaves held in the areas of the South that were not at that time under Federal control. It expressly excluded the slaves in the Northern and Border States, in designated counties and parishes of Virginia and Louisiana, and in the entire State of Tennessee, all of which were under Union occupation. The condition of slaves in these latter regions was left "precisely as if this proclamation were not issued." As Secretary of State Seward bitterly complained, "We show our sympathy with slavery by emancipating slaves where we cannot reach them and holding them in bondage where we can set them free."[14] The editor of the Democratic *New York World* likewise pointed out on January 3, 1863 that:

> The President has purposely made the proclamation inoperative in all places where we have gained a military footing which makes the slaves accessible. He has proclaimed emancipation only where he has notoriously no power to execute it. The exemption of the accessible parts of Louisiana, Tennessee, and Virginia renders the proclamation not merely futile, but ridiculous.
>
> Immediate practical effect it has none; the slaves remaining in precisely the same condition as before. They still live on the plantations, tenant their accustomed hovels, obey the command of their master . . . and doing the work he requires precisely as though Mr. Lincoln had not declared them free. . . . So long, therefore, as the

13. Letter to Hon. James C. Conkling, August 26, 1863; Basler, ibid., Volume VI, page 406.

14. Piatt, *Men Who Saved the Union*, page 150.

present status continues, the freedom declared by this proclamation is a dormant, not an actual freedom.[15]

George E. Stephens, a sergeant of the all-Black 54th Massachusetts Volunteers, denounced "the false and indefinite policy of the Administration" for leaving slavery untouched in the Border States and described the proclamation as "an abortion wrung from the Executive womb by necessity" and "the fulmination of one man, by virtue of his military authority, who proposes to free the slaves of that portion of territory over which he has no control, while those portions of slave territory under control of the Union armies is exempted, and slavery receives as much protection as it ever did." Stephens further complained that "United States officers and soldiers are yet employed hunting fugitive slaves."[16] Frederick Douglass noted that "it was not a proclamation of 'liberty throughout all the land, unto all the inhabitants thereof,' such as we had hoped it would be, but was one marked by discriminations and reservations. Its operation was confined within certain geographical and military lines. It only abolished slavery where it did not exist, and left it intact where it did exist. It was a measure apparently inspired by the low motive of military necessity, and by so far as it was so, it would become inoperative and useless when military necessity should cease."[17]

---

15. James G. Randall, *The Civil War and Reconstruction* (Boston: D.C. Heath and Company, 1937), page 491.

16. *New York Weekly Anglo-African*, September 1864; Donald Yacovone (editor), *A Voice of Thunder: A Black Soldier's Civil War* (Chicago: University of Illinois Press, 1998), page 324.

17. Douglass, *Life and Times of Douglass*, page 256.

Lincoln's primary motive in issuing the Emancipation Proclamation was clear from what he had written to Greeley: "What I do in regard to slavery, and the colored race, I do because I believe it helps to save the Union." Up to this point, he had always been careful to keep the issue of slavery out of the war, but after a year and a half of bloodshed, it had become obvious that the South was thoroughly committed to vindicating its independence, and thus conquest by any means necessary was required. As Lincoln would later recall: "Things had gone on from bad to worse, until I felt that we had reached the end of our rope on the plan of operations we had been pursuing; that we had about played our last card, and must change our tactics, or lose the game! I now determined upon the adoption of the emancipation policy."[18] The proclamation, initially issued on September 22, 1862, would take effect on January 1, 1863 should the Southern States still be in arms against the North. However, if Southerners surrendered before the new year, the proclamation would be inoperative and their States would be restored to the Union with their domestic institutions intact.

The secondary purpose of the proclamation was believed by many to have been to incite widespread slave rebellions throughout the South, thereby forcing the withdrawal of troops from the war to restore order at home. Such was not an unfounded fear, for Lincoln himself had announced that, in the event of a forced emancipation of the slaves, he had no objections "of a moral nature in view

---

18. Statement to Francis Carpenter on February 6, 1864; Francis B. Carpenter, *The Inner Life of Abraham Lincoln: Six Months at the White House* (New York: Hurd and Houghton, 1867), page 20.

of possible consequences of insurrection and massacre at the South."[19] Many of the Northern radicals were quite vocal in their advocacy of servile insurrection "as a punishment for the seceding States."[20] This bloodthirsty attitude was best exemplified by Charles Sumner in a speech delivered at Fanueil Hall in Boston on October 6, 1862: "I know of no principle of war or of reason even by which our Rebels should be saved from the natural consequences of their own conduct. When they rose against a paternal government they set an example of insurrection which has carried death to innumerable firesides. They cannot complain, if their slaves, with better reason, follow it. According to an old law, bloody inventions return to plague the inventor."[21] The editors of the *North American Review* of Boston opined, "It may be that the slaves thus armed will commit some atrocities. . . . We hesitate not to say, that it will be better, immeasurably better, that the rebellion should be crushed, even with the incidental consequences attendant on a servile insurrection, than that the hopes of the world in the capacity of mankind to maintain free institutions should expire with American liberty."[22]

That a slave uprising was actually planned by the au-

19. Nicolay and Hay, *Lincoln: Complete Works*, Volume II, page 234.

20. Rhodes, *History of the United States*, Volume IV, page 344; Welles, *Diary of Gideon Welles*, Volume II, pages 277-278.

21. Charles Sumner, *The Works of Charles Sumner* (Boston: Lee and Shepherd, 1880), Volume VII, page 226. Ironically, the venue in which the radical Abolitionist Sumner spoke these words had been gifted to the city of Boston in 1742 by the wealthy slavetrader, Peter Faneuil.

22. Joel Parker, "The Character of the Rebellion and the Conduct of the War," *North American Review* (Cambridge: Welch, Bigelow, and Company, 1862), October 1862, pages 532-533.

thorities in Washington was verified when a secret dispatch from Augustus S. Montgomery to Major General John G. Foster was discovered in the summer of 1863, which directed commanders "in each military department in the seceded States" to "induce the Blacks to make a simultaneous movement of rising, on the night of the 1st of August next, over the entire States in rebellion, to arm themselves with any and every kind of weapon that may come to hand, and commence operations by burning all the railroad and country bridges, and tear up the railroad tracks, and to destroy telegraph lines, etc., and then take to the woods, swamps, or the mountains, where they may emerge as occasion may offer for provisions and for further depredations."[23] Of course, that no insurrection of any notable extent ever occurred during the entire war is attributable to the mutual feelings of kindness that existed between the races in the South at that time — a familial relationship between master and slave that was inconceivable to the Northern mind:

> . . . [S]o far as the people of the South are concerned, [the Negro slave] sustained the armies of the Confederacy during the great Civil War. . . . There was not a day during the trying period of the Civil War when he might not have disbanded the Southern armies. An outbreak on his part against the defenseless homes of the South would have occasioned the utter dissolution of the Southern armies, and turned the anx-

23. *Official Records*, Series I, Volume LI, Part II, page 736. This directive did contain the added proviso that the slaves refrain from violence, but it is difficult to understand how such was to be prevented if the Blacks had been so inclined.

ious faces of the veterans in gray toward their homes. But no Southern soldier ever dreamed of the possibility of a condition like this. So far as his home was concerned, it was not any apprehension of the unfaithfulness of the slaves which occasioned the slightest alarm.[24]

Finally, there was also a political purpose behind the Emancipation Proclamation. Some nations in Europe, especially Great Britain, were on the verge of extending diplomatic recognition to the Confederacy and Lincoln hoped that a "bold declaration of an antislavery policy" would rally the European liberal parties to oppose any such gestures by their governments.[25] In his reply to the Abolitionist clergy of Chicago on September 13, 1862, he wrote, ". . . [T]o proclaim emancipation would secure the sympathy of Europe and the whole civilized world, which now saw no other reason for the strife than national pride and am-

---

24. Benjamin Franklin Riley, *The White Man's Burden: A Discussion of the Interracial Question With Special Reference to the Responsibility of the White Race to the Negro Problem* (Birmingham, Alabama: self-published, 1910), pages 63-64.

25. Williams, *Lincoln and the Radicals*, page 169. Proof of a strong pro-Southern sentiment among British conservatives may be seen in James Spence's *On the Recognition of the Southern Confederation* (London: Richard Bentley, 1862) and *The American Union: Its Effect on National Character and Policy With an Enquiry Into Secession as a Constitutional Right and the Causes of Disruption* (London: Richard Bentley, 1862), and Charles Dickens' two-part essay on the American conflict which appeared in the December 21 and 28, 1862 issues of *All The Year Round, A Weekly Journal* (London: Chapman and Hall, 1862), Volume VI, Numbers 140, 141. See also Donald Bellows, "A Study of British Conservative Reaction to the American Civil War," *The Journal of Southern History*, Volume LI, Number 4 (November, 1985), pages 505-526.

bition, an unwillingness to abridge our domain and power. No other step would be so potent to prevent foreign intervention."[26] Woodrow Wilson in his *History of the American People* translated this sophistry as follows: "It was necessary to put the South at a moral disadvantage by transforming the contest from a war waged against States fighting for their independence into a war against States fighting for the maintenance and extension of slavery, by making some open move for emancipation as the real motive of the struggle. Once make the war a struggle against slavery, and the world, it might be hoped, would see it a moral war, not a political; and the sympathy of nations would begin to run for the North, not for the South."[27] The British, however, were not easily fooled by the transparent propaganda. Calling the proclamation "a deceitful fabrication," the *London Spectator* noted, "The Government liberates the enemy's slaves as it would the enemy's cattle, simply to weaken them in the coming conflict. . . . The principle asserted is not that a human being cannot justly own another, but that he cannot own him unless he is loyal to the United States."[28] Likewise, British foreign minister Earl John Russell commented, "The Proclamation of the President of the United States . . . appears to be of a very strange nature. It professes to emancipate all slaves in places where the United States authorities cannot exercise any jurisdiction . . . but it does not decree emancipation . . . in any States, or parts of

---

26. Basler, *Collected Works of Lincoln*, Volume V, page 421.

27. Woodrow Wilson, *A History of the American People* (New York: Harper and Brothers, Publishers, 1901), Volume IV, page 231.

28. *London Spectator*, October 11, 1862, page 1125; Rhodes, *History of the United States*), Volume IV, page 344.

States, occupied by federal troops. . . . There seems to be no declaration of a principle adverse to slavery in this proclamation. It is a measure of war, and a measure of war of a very questionable kind."[29]

Virtually no one at the time believed, as do modern Americans, that Lincoln "freed the slaves." The Emancipation Proclamation was not, nor was it designed to be, a humanitarian measure. As one historian noted, "So famous has this proclamation become, and so encrusted with tradition, that a correct historical conception of its actual effect is rarely found in the voluminous literature which the subject has evoked. The stereotyped picture of the emancipator suddenly striking the shackles from millions of slaves by a stroke of the presidential pen is altogether inaccurate."[30] Instead, the only slaves that the proclamation actually freed were those who voluntarily came into Union lines, and those captured by the Northern armies in their movement southward.[31] These Negroes were compelled to

---

29. Letter to British consul Lord Richard Lyons, January 17, 1863; Henry Wheaton, *Elements of International Law* (Boston: Little, Brown and Company, 1863), page 37.

30. Randall, *Civil War and Reconstruction*, page 490.

31. Of the estimated 186,000 Blacks who served the Union army in some capacity, a great many had been kidnaped from Southern plantations. The Government records contain numerous communications between military and government officials regarding this fact. For example, Edward L. Pierce, who had been appointed to create schools and hospitals for former slaves in Port Royal, South Carolina, reported on May 13, 1862 that, "On some plantations the wailing and screaming were loud and the women threw themselves in despair on the ground. On some plantations the people took to the woods and were hunted up by the soldiers. . . . I doubt if the recruiting service in this country has ever been attended with such scenes before" (*Official*

serve as an auxiliary work force of cooks, ditch diggers, teamsters, laundresses, and seamstresses, and some were later organized into combat troops. Those who were not deemed useful to the war effort were confined in "contraband camps," which were invariably disease-ridden with high mortality rates. The bigoted Northern soldiers were often very abusive toward the Blacks, and assaults, rapes, and even murders were frequently committed and regularly went unpunished.[32] So bad had the situation become that, in the words of one soldier, it "created a suspicion that the Government has not the interest in the negroes that it has professed, and many of them sighed yesterday for the 'old fetters' as being better than the new liberty."[33]

The Emancipation Proclamation was merely a "a practical war measure" that, by Lincoln's own admission, rested entirely on military necessity: "Understand, I raise no objections against it on legal or constitutional grounds; for, as commander-in-chief of the army and navy, in time of war, I suppose I have a right to take any measure which may best subdue the enemy. . . ."[34] Two years after its issuance, he was still doubtful of both the legality and effectiveness

Records, Series III, Volume II, page 57). General John A. Logan likewise reported on February 26, 1864, "A major of the colored troops is here with his party capturing negroes, with or without their consent. . . . [T]hey are being conscripted" (ibid., Series I, Volume XXXII, Part II, page 477). See Appendix Three.

32. Ibid., Series I, Volume III, page 459; Series I, Volume XIV, page 376; Series I
Part III, page 1005; Series III, Volume IV, page 1029.

33. G. M. Wells to Edward Pierce, May 13, 1862; ibid., Series III, Volume II, page 59

34. Basler, *Collected Works of Lincoln*, Volume V, page 421.

of the proclamation: "A question might be raised whether the proclamation was legally valid.[35] It might be urged, that it only aided those that came into our lines, and that it was inoperative as to those who did not give themselves up; or that it would have had no effect upon the children of slaves born hereafter; in fact, it would be urged that it did not meet the evil."[36] On another occasion, he expressed his concern that the proclamation would be no more effective toward granting the slaves freedom than "the Pope's bull against the comet."[37] When meeting with Confederate

---

35. This question was indeed raised by Benjamin Robbins Curtis, a Supreme Court justice who had previously dissented from the majority opinion in the famous *Dred Scott v. Sandford* case of 1857:

> This proclamation . . . by an executive decree, proposes to repeal and annul valid State laws which regulate the domestic relations of their people. . . .
>
> It must be obvious to the meanest capacity, that if the President of the United States has an implied constitutional right, as commander-in-chief of the army and navy in time of war, to disregard any one positive prohibition of the Constitution, or to exercise any one power not delegated to the United States by the Constitution, because, in his judgment, he may thereby "best subdue the enemy," he has the same right, for the same reason, to disregard each and every provision of the Constitution, and to exercise all power, needful, in his opinion, to enable him "best to subdue the enemy". . . .
>
> The necessary result of this interpretation of the Constitution is, that, in time of war, the President has any and all power, which he may deem it necessary to exercise, to subdue the enemy; and that . . . every right reserved to the States or the people, rests merely upon executive discretion (*Executive Power* [Boston: Little, Brown and Company, 1862], pages 15, 18).

36. Basler, *Collected Works of Lincoln*, Volume VIII, page 254.

37. Reply to the Emancipation Memorial from the religious leaders of Chicago, September 15, 1862; Basler, ibid., Volume V, page 420.

dignitaries at the Hampton Roads peace conference on February 3, 1865, Lincoln said that the proclamation "would have effect only from its being an exercise of the war power," and "as soon as the war ceased, it would be inoperative for the future." Furthermore, "it would be held to apply only to such slaves as had come under its operation while it was in active exercise"[38] — leaving in bondage the slaves in those areas of the South and throughout the Border States that the proclamation had specifically exempted.[39] Certainly, then, if Lincoln had actually "freed the slaves," as he is often credited with doing, there would have been no need for the Thirteenth Amendment.

---

38. Alexander H. Stephens, *A Constitutional View of the War Between the States* (Philadelphia, Pennsylvania: National Publishing Company, 1870), Volume II, page 611.

39. One of the latter was the slave State of West Virginia, which Lincoln's signature had admitted to the Union on June 20, 1863.

APPENDIX ONE

The Emancipation Proclamation

By the President of the United States of America:
A Proclamation.

Whereas, on the twenty-second day of September, in the year of our Lord one thousand eight hundred and sixty-two, a proclamation was issued by the President of the United States, containing, among other things, the following, to wit:

"That on the first day of January, in the year of our Lord one thousand eight hundred and sixty-three, all persons held as slaves within any State or designated parts of a State, the people whereof shall then be in rebellion against the United States, shall be then, thenceforward, and forever free; and the Executive Government of the United States, including the military and naval authority thereof, will recognize and maintain the freedom of such persons, and will do no act or acts to repress such persons, or any of them, in any efforts they may make for their actual freedom.

"That the Executive will, on the first day of January

aforesaid, by proclamation, designate the States and parts of States, if any, in which the people thereof, respectively, shall then be in rebellion against the United States; and the fact that any State, or the people thereof, shall on that day be, in good faith, represented in the Congress of the United States by members chosen thereto at elections wherein a majority of the qualified voters of such State shall have participated, shall, in the absence of strong countervailing testimony, be deemed conclusive evidence that such State, and the people thereof, are not then in rebellion against the United States."

Now, therefore I, Abraham Lincoln, President of the United States, by virtue of the power in me vested as Commander-in-Chief, of the Army and Navy of the United States in time of actual armed rebellion against the authority and government of the United States, and as a fit and necessary war measure for suppressing said rebellion, do, on this first day of January, in the year of our Lord one thousand eight hundred and sixty-three, and in accordance with my purpose so to do publicly proclaimed for the full period of one hundred days, from the day first above mentioned, order and designate as the States and parts of States wherein the people thereof respectively, are this day in rebellion against the United States, the following, to wit:

Arkansas, Texas, Louisiana, (except the Parishes of St. Bernard, Plaquemines, Jefferson, St. John, St. Charles, St. James Ascension, Assumption, Terrebonne, Lafourche, St. Mary, St. Martin, and Orleans, including the City of New Orleans) Mississippi, Alabama, Florida, Georgia, South Carolina, North Carolina, and Virginia, (except the fortyeight counties designated as West Virginia, and also the counties of Berkley, Accomac, Northampton, Elizabeth City, York,

Princess Ann, and Norfolk, including the cities of Norfolk and Portsmouth), and which excepted parts, are for the present, left precisely as if this proclamation were not issued.

And by virtue of the power, and for the purpose aforesaid, I do order and declare that all persons held as slaves within said designated States, and parts of States, are, and henceforward shall be free; and that the Executive government of the United States, including the military and naval authorities thereof, will recognize and maintain the freedom of said persons.

And I hereby enjoin upon the people so declared to be free to abstain from all violence, unless in necessary self-defence; and I recommend to them that, in all cases when allowed, they labor faithfully for reasonable wages.

And I further declare and make known, that such persons of suitable condition, will be received into the armed service of the United States to garrison forts, positions, stations, and other places, and to man vessels of all sorts in said service.

And upon this act, sincerely believed to be an act of justice, warranted by the Constitution, upon military necessity, I invoke the considerate judgment of mankind, and the gracious favor of Almighty God.

In witness whereof, I have hereunto set my hand and caused the seal of the United States to be affixed.

Done at the City of Washington, this first day of January, in the year of our Lord one thousand eight hundred and sixty three, and of the Independence of the United States of America the eighty-seventh.

By the President: ABRAHAM LINCOLN
WILLIAM H. SEWARD, Secretary of State.

APPENDIX TWO
The Original Thirteenth Amendment

Most Americans are familiar with the Thirteenth Amendment which became part of the U.S. Constitution on December 6, 1865: "Neither slavery nor involuntary servitude, except as a punishment for crime whereof the party shall have been duly convicted, shall exist within the United States, or any place subject to their jurisdiction." Not as well known is the existence of another amendment, also numbered the thirteenth, which Congress passed nearly five years earlier: "No amendment shall be made to the Constitution which will authorize or give to Congress the power to abolish or interfere, within any State, with the domestic institutions thereof, including that of persons held to labor or service by the laws of the said State."[1]

At the request of outgoing President James Buchanan, this amendment bill was introduced in the House of Representatives by Thomas Corwin of Ohio and in the Senate

---

1. Edward McPherson, *The Political History of the United States of America, During the Great Rebellion* (Washington, D.C.: Philip and Solomons, 1865), page 71.

by future Secretary of State William Seward[2] — notably, both sponsors were Republicans. The intended purpose of the bill was to induce the seceded States to rejoin the Union, and to encourage the Border States to remain. One month after the secession of the last Cotton State (Texas), and three weeks after the formation of the new provisional Confederate Government in Montgomery, Alabama, the "Corwin Amendment," as it came to be known, was passed by both houses of the Thirty-Sixth Congress on March 2, 1861[3] and thereafter signed by Buchanan. In his first Inaugural Address, Lincoln gave his verbal support to this amendment: "I understand a proposed amendment to the Constitution – which amendment, however, I have not seen – has passed Congress, to the effect that the Federal Government shall never interfere with the domestic institutions of the States, including that of persons held to service . . . holding such a provision to now be implied constitutional law, I have no objection to its being made express and irrevocable." On March 16, 1861, Lincoln forwarded a copy of the amendment to the Governors of all the States, including those which had already seceded, noting its endorsement by his predecessor.[4] The seceded States completely ignored the measure, but it was thereafter ratified

---

2. *The Statutes at Large, Treaties and Proclamations of the United States of America, From December 5, 1859 to March 3, 1863* (Boston: Little, Brown and Company, 1863), Volume XII, page 251.

3. 46 of the 133 affirmative votes in the House, and 9 of the 24 affirmative votes in the Senate, were cast by Republicans.

4. John A. Lupton, "Abraham Lincoln and the Corwin Amendment," *Illinois Heritage* (September-October 2006), Volume IX, Number 5, page 34.

by five Union States: Kentucky, Ohio, Rhode Island, Maryland, and Illinois, and also by the rump Virginia legislature in Wheeling that would later be admitted to the Union as the slave State of West Virginia.

Of course, there was really nothing extraordinary in the wording of this proposed amendment, for it merely reiterated the principle already stated in the Tenth Amendment that Congress could not go beyond its specifically enumerated powers to encroach upon the reserved powers of the States. As previously discussed, this political maxim had been embodied in the 1860 Republican platform and was repeatedly acknowledged by Lincoln himself. Seward likewise said in his "Union" speech in the Senate on January 14, 1861:

> Experience in public affairs has confirmed my opinion, that domestic slavery, existing in any State, is wisely left by the Constitution of the United States exclusively to the care, management, and disposition of that State; and if it were in my power, I would not alter the Constitution in that respect. If misapprehension of my position needs so strong a remedy, I am willing to vote for an amendment to the Constitution, declaring that it shall not, by any future amendment, be so altered so as to confer on Congress a power to abolish or interfere with slavery in any State.[5]

One writer noted that, in the standard history books, "The [original] amendment gets no more than cursory treat-

---

5. *Congressional Globe*, Thirty-Sixth Congress, Second Session, page 344. In this speech, Seward also stated his position that the Fugitive Slave Law must be enforced.

ment, fuzzy on specific details and at points simply misin-
formed."[6] The reason for this neglect is understandable in
light of the fact that the existence of the amendment cre-
ates a major problem for the commonly accepted narrative
that the Southern States seceded and subsequently waged
war against the North for the sole purpose of protecting
slavery. The product of a Republican-dominated Congress,
the "Corwin Amendment" offered precisely this protection, whereas secession eliminated all constitutional guarantees and placed slavery in the very path of destruction.[7]

On February 8, 1864, as the prospects of a Union victory over the Confederacy were improving, a resolution to
withdraw the amendment was introduced in the Senate by
Republican Henry B. Anthony of Rhode Island and referred
to the Judiciary Committee for consideration. No further
action was taken and the resolution was finally discharged
three months later, leaving the amendment an open question throughout the remainder of the war. If it had been
ratified by the required number of States prior to 1865, the
later Thirteenth, Fourteenth, and Fifteenth Amendments
would have never existed.

An interesting endnote to this subject is the little-
known fact that the amendment remained dormant for a

---

6. Daniel W. Crofts, *Lincoln and the Politics of Slavery: The Other Thirteenth Amendment and the Struggle to Save the Union* (Chapel Hill, North
Carolina, University of North Carolina Press, 2016), page 9.

7. Many of the radical Abolitionists (Garrison, Phillips, et. al) had
realized the safety of slavery within the Union and had therefore become staunch advocates of Southern secession as a means to destroy
the institution. It is likely that the main purpose of their decades-long
agitation of the slavery question was to exasperate the South into
finally withdrawing from the Union.

century until a resolution to ratify was introduced in the Texas House of Representatives on March 7, 1963 by Republican Henry Stollenwerck of Dallas. The Maryland legislature rescinded the State's former ratification on April 7, 2014. Until it is completely removed from the books, the "Corwin Amendment" could still become part of the Constitution if ratified by the requisite number of States.

APPENDIX THREE

The Conscription of Southern Blacks

Much has been made by modern revisionist historians of the fact that an estimated 186,000 Blacks fought under the United States flag against the South.[1] However, we are seldom, if ever, told the reason for this. According to William Whiting of Massachusetts, who served as solicitor of the War Department from 1862 to 1865, "All the property of rebels [is] forfeited to the treasury of the country," and "slave property [is] subject to the same liability as other property to be appropriated for war purposes."[2] Lincoln's second Secretary of War, Edwin Stanton, elaborated on this premise: "The population of African descent that cultivate the lands and perform the labor of the rebels constitute a large share of their military strength, and enable the white masters to fill the rebel armies and wage a cruel and murderous war against the people of the Northern States. By

---

1. *Official Records*, Series III, Volume V, page 661.

2. William Whiting, *The War Powers of the President* (Boston: John L. Shorey, 1862), pages 28, 107.

reducing the laboring strength of the rebels their military power will be reduced."[3] Consequently, the invading Northern army began to seize Southern slaves and conscript them into service, often against their will. On March 6, 1863, General Orders 17, from the Department of the South headquarters at Hilton Head, South Carolina, stipulated:

> [A]ll able-bodied male negroes between the ages of eighteen and fifty within the military lines of the Department of the South who are not, on the day of the date of this order, regularly and permanently employed in the quartermaster and commissary departments, or as the private servants of officers, within the allowance made by the Army Regulations, are hereby drafted into the military service of the United States, to serve as non-commissioned officers and soldiers in the various regiments and brigades now organized, and in process of being organized, by Brig. Gen. Rufus Saxton, specially authorized to raise such troops by orders of the War Department.[4]

After this order had failed to produce the desired results, an amended order was issued on August 16, 1864:

> In view of the necessities of the military service, the want of recruits to complete the unfilled regiments in this department, the great numbers of unemployed colored men and deserters hiding about to avoid labor or service, and in consideration of the large bounties now

---

3. Dispatch to Brigadier-General Rufus Saxton, August 25, 1862; *Official Records*, Series I, Volume XIV, pages 377-378.

4. Ibid., Volume XIV, page 1020.

paid to volunteers by the Government, General Orders, No. 17, dated headquarters Department of the South, Hilton Head, S.C., March 6, 1863, is hereby amended to read as follows:

All able-bodied colored men between the ages of eighteen and fifty, within the military lines of the Department of the South, who have had an opportunity to enlist voluntarily and refused to do so, shall be drafted into the military service of the United States. . . .

The owners or superintendents of plantations, and all other persons throughout the department not in the military service, are hereby authorized and required to arrest and deliver to the local provost-marshal of the nearest military post all deserters in their employ or loitering about their plantations, and if it be necessary for a guard to make the arrest, it shall be the duty of such person or persons knowing of the whereabouts of any deserter, or person by common reports called a deserter, to report the fact to the nearest military commander, and also to render him all assistance in his power to cause the arrest. Any person found guilty of violating this section shall be severely punished.[5]

These orders adequately account for a large majority of the Black men who bore arms against their former masters, without whom Lincoln declared that he would have to "abandon the war in three weeks."[6] In a February 26, 1864 dispatch from Huntsville, Alabama, General John A. Logan wrote that "a major of colored troops is here with his party capturing negroes, with or without their consent.

---

5. General Orders 119; ibid., Series III, Volume IV, page 621.

6. Nicolay and Hay, *Lincoln: Complete Works*, Volume II, page 562.

... [T]hey are being conscripted."[7] On September 1, 1864, Captain Frederick Martin reported from New Berne, North Carolina, "The negroes will not go voluntarily, so I am obliged to force them. . . . I expect to get a large lot to-morrow."[8] To this report, General Innis N. Palmer added:

> The matter of collecting the colored men for laborers has been one of some difficulty, but I hope to send up a respectable force. The matter has been fairly explained to the contrabands, and they have been treated with the utmost consideration, but they will not go willingly. Now, I take it that the state of the country needs their services, and that if they will not go willingly they must be forced to go, and I propose to take all I can find who are in no permanent employment and send them up. I am aware that this may be considered a harsh measure, but at such a time we must not stop at trifles.[9]

In the words of General Rufus A. Saxton, "Men have been seized and forced to enlist who had large families of young children dependent upon them for support and fine crops of cotton and corn nearly ready for harvest, without an opportunity of making provision for the one or securing the other." On at least one occasion, "three boys, one only fourteen years of age, were seized in a field where they were at work and sent to a regiment serving in a distant part of the department without the knowledge of

---

7. John A. Logan to T.S. Bowers, February 26, 1864; *Official Records*, Series I, Volume XXXII, Part II, page 477.

8. Frederick Martin to Benjamin F. Butler, September 1, 1864; ibid., Series I, Volume XLII, Part II, pages 653-654.

9. Innis N. Palmer to R.S. Davis, September 1, 1864; ibid., page 654.

their parents. . . ."[10] It was also reported that, "On some plantations the wailing and screaming were loud and the women threw themselves in despair on the ground. On some plantations the people took to the woods and were hunted up by the soldiers. . . . I doubt if the recruiting service in this country has ever been attended with such scenes before."[11]

It was not uncommon for these Black regiments to be "forced to the front by a wall of bayonets, in white hands, behind them."[12] One Northern soldier is quoted as saying, "I used to be opposed to having black troops, but when I saw ten cart-loads of dead niggers carried off the field yesterday I thought it better they should be killed than I."[13] Another soldier commented that this treatment "has created a suspicion that the Government has not the interest in the negroes that it has professed, and many of them sighed yesterday for the 'old fetters' as being better than the new liberty."[14] Some slaves, supposedly emancipated by Lincoln's proclamation of January 1, 1863, even found themselves traded back to Southern planters by Northern officers in exchange for cotton. One Government document revealed:

---

10. Rufus A. Saxton to Edwin M. Stanton, December 30, 1864, ibid., Series III, Volume IV, page 1028.

11. Edward L. Pierce to David Hunter May 13, 1862; ibid., Series III, Volume II, page 57.

12. Carpenter, *Logic of History*, page 170.

13. Charles Godfrey Leland, *Abraham Lincoln* (New York: G. P. Putnam's Sons, 1881), page 61.

14. G. M. Wells to Edward Pierce, May 13, 1862; *Official Records*, Series III, Volume II, page 59.

A commission is now in session at the west with Maj. Gen. McDowell at its head, investigating the conduct of Maj. Gen. [Samuel R.] Curtis and other Republican officials, in conducting their military operations so as to secure the largest amount of cotton possible for their own private benefit. One of the richest revelations made is in reference to the trading off of negroes for cotton! The specification alleges that negro slaves had been taken from the plantations upon the pretense of giving them freedom under the President's "emancipation edict," and thus used as a substitute for coin. It has been fully proven before the investigating court. The officer charged with this lucrative speculation was Col. [Charles E.] Hovey of Illinois, formerly the principal of the State Normal School at Bloomington.[15]

Because the invading Northern soldiers had been instructed to view the Southern slaves as "enemy property," to be confiscated and appropriated to the use of the United States Army, it was inevitable that the hatred these men carried in their hearts toward the people of the South would be projected upon their helpless servants. In his December 7, 1863 address to the Confederate Congress, Jefferson Davis stated:

Nor has less unrelenting warfare been waged by these pretended friends of human rights and liberties against the unfortunate negroes. Wherever the enemy

15. Carpenter, *Logic of History*, page 263. See United States War Department, Court-Martial Cases, 1809-1894, Judge Advocate General Records, Record Group 153 (Washington, D.C.: National Archives) Court of Inquiry of Major General Samuel R. Curtis (KK-885), Boxes 406-407 (microfilm copy), reel 1:36.

have been able to gain access they have forced into the ranks of their army every able-bodied man that they could seize, and have either left the aged, the women, and the children to perish by starvation, or have gathered them into camps where they have been wasted by a frightful mortality. Without clothing or shelter, often without food, incapable without supervision of taking the most ordinary precautions against disease, these helpless dependents, accustomed to have their wants supplied by the foresight of their masters, are being rapidly exterminated wherever brought in contact with the invaders. By the Northern man, on whose deep-rooted prejudices no kindly restraining influence is exercised, they are treated with aversion and neglect. There is little hazard in predicting that in all localities where the enemy have gained a temporary foothold the negroes, who under our care increased six-fold in number since their importation into the colonies by Great Britain, will have been reduced by mortality during the war to no more than one half their previous number.

Information on this subject is derived not only from our own observation and from the reports of the negroes who succeed in escaping from the enemy, but full confirmation is afforded by statements published in the Northern journals by humane persons engaged in making appeals to the charitable for aid in preventing the ravages of disease, exposure, and starvation among the negro women and children who are crowded into encampments.[16]

Davis' words are easily verified. Indeed, the official records of the war, published by the United States Govern-

---

16. *Official Records*, Series IV, Volume II, Part I, page 1047.

ment, are literally filled with accounts of the robbery, rape, and murder endured by Southern Blacks at the hands of their supposed "liberators." General Orders 27, issued on August 17, 1862 under the authority of Major-General David Hunter, stated that "numerous acts of pilfering from the negroes have taken place in the neighborhood of Beaufort, committed by men wearing the uniform of the United States."[17] J.T.K. Hayward testified that Northern soldiers were "committing rapes on the negroes and such like things. . . . and no punishment, or none of any account, has been meted out to them."[18] In the tiny town of Athens, Alabama, Northern soldiers under the command of Colonel John B. Turchin "attempted an indecent outrage on [a] servant girl," and quartered themselves "in the negro huts for weeks, debauching the females." This account also tells of the gang-rape "on the person of a colored girl. . . ."[19] Although Turchin was court-martialed and convicted for these crimes on July 7, 1862, he was promoted by Lincoln only a month later to the rank of brigadier general.[20]

The following letter dated December 29, 1862 was written by a Northern chaplain and two surgeons stationed at Helena, Arkansas:

> The undersigned Chaplains and Surgeons of the army of the Eastern District of Arkansas would respectfully call your attention to the Statements and Suggestions following. The contrabands within our lines are ex-

---

17. Ibid., Series I, Volume XIV, page 376.

18. Ibid., Series I, Volume III, page 459.

19. Ibid., Series I, Volume XVI, Part II, pages 273-275.

20. Ibid., page 277.

periencing hardships, oppression and neglect the removal of which calls loudly for the intervention of authority. We daily see and deplore the evil and leave it to
your wisdom to devise a remedy. In a great degree the
contrabands are left entirely to the mercy and rapacity
of the unprincipled part of our army (excepting only the
limited jurisdiction of Capt. Richmond) with no person
clothed with specific authority to look after and protect
them. Among the list of grievances we mention these:

Some who have been paid by individuals for cotton
or for labor have been waylaid by soldiers, robbed, and
in several instances fired upon, as well as robbed, and
in no case that we can now recall have the plunderers
been brought to justice.

The wives of some have been molested by soldiers
to gratify their licentious lust, and their husbands murdered in endeavoring to defend them, and yet the guilty
parties, though known, were not arrested. Some who
have wives and families are required to work on the
fortifications, or to unload Government stores, and receive only their meals at the public table, while their
families, whatever provision is intended for them, are,
as a matter of fact, left in a helpless and starving condition.

Many of the contrabands have been employed, and
received in numerous instances, from officers and pri-
vates, only counterfeit money or nothing at all for their
services. One man was employed as a teamster by the
Government and he died in the service (the Government indebted to him nearly fifty dollars) leaving an
orphan child eight years old, and there is no apparent
provision made to draw the money, or to care for the
orphan child. The negro hospital here has become noto-
rious for filth, neglect, mortality and brutal whipping,

so that the contrabands have lost all hope of kind treatment there, and would almost as soon go to their graves as to their hospital. These grievances reported to us by persons in whom we have confidence, and some of which we know to be true, are but a few of the many wrongs of which they complain.

For the sake of humanity, for the sake of Christianity, for the good name of our army, for the honor of our country, cannot something be done to prevent this oppression and stop its demoralizing influences upon the soldiers themselves? Some have suggested that the matter be laid before the Department at Washington, in the hope that they will clothe an agent with authority to register all the names of the contrabands, who will have a benevolent regard for their welfare, through whom all details of fatigue and working parties shall be made, through whom rations may be drawn and money paid, and who shall be empowered to organize schools, and to make all needful regulations for the comfort and improvement of the condition of the contrabands; whose accounts shall be open at all times for inspection, and who shall make stated reports to the Department.

All which is respectfully submitted,

Samuel Sawyer
Pearl P. Ingall
J.G. Forman[21]

---

21. Samuel Sawyer, et al. to Maj. Gen. Curtis, December 29, 1862, enclosed in Chaplain Samuel Sawyer to Major Gen. Curtis, January 26, 1863, #135 1863, Letters Received Relating to Military Discipline & Control, series 22, Headquarters of the Army, Record Group 108, National Archives; Ira Berlin, Barbara J. Fields, Steven F. Miller, Joseph P. Reidy, and Leslie S. Rowland (editors), *Free at Last: A Documentary History of Slavery, Freedom, and the Civil War* (New York: The New Press, 1992), pages 180-182.

After the fall of Richmond, Virginia, General Grant was notified that "a number of cases of atrocious rape by these men have already occurred. Their influence on the colored population is also reported to be bad."[22] General Saxton wrote the following report to Secretary of War Stanton on December 30, 1864: "I found the prejudice of color and race here in full force, and the general feeling of the army of occupation was unfriendly to the blacks. It was manifested in various forms of personal insult and abuse, in depredations on their plantations, stealing and destroying their crops and domestic animals, and robbing them of their money. . . . The women were held as the legitimate prey of lust. . . ."[23] Private John W. Haley of the Seventeenth Maine Regiment, related how he and his fellow soldiers amused themselves at the Negroes' expense: "A host of young niggers followed us to camp and soon made themselves too familiar. We bounced them up in blankets and made them butt against each other also against some pork barrels and hard-bread boxes. A couple hours worth of bouncing satisfied them. One young nigger had an arm broke and several others were more or less maltreated."[24] The *Official Records* also record the following November 26, 1862 communiqué from General John A. Dix: " . . . [T]he colored people . . . have been forced to remain all night on the wharf without shelter and without food; . . . one has died, and . . . others

---

22. Henry W. Halleck to Ulysses S. Grant, April 29, 1865; *Official Records*, Series I, Volume XLVI, Part III, page 1005.

23. Ibid., Series III, Volume IV, page 1029.

24. Ruth L. Silliker (editor), *The Rebel Yell and Yankee Hurrah: The Civil War Journal of a Maine Volunteer* (Camden, Maine: Down East Books, 1985), page 273.

are suffering with disease and . . . your men have turned them out of their houses, which they have built themselves, and have robbed some of them of their money and personal effects."[25]

Such accounts were corroborated by the eyewitness testimonies of Southerners themselves, both White and Black. The vast majority of atrocities against the Negroes were committed by Northern soldiers during William T. Sherman's infamous march from Atlanta, Georgia to Charleston, South Carolina in late 1864 and early 1865. Mrs. Nora Canning of Savannah, Georgia told how the dead baby of one of the family's slave-women was dug up by Northern soldiers looking for buried treasure, the body being carelessly cast aside "for the hog to root" when none was found.[26] Dr. Daniel Trezevant, a respected citizen of Columbia, South Carolina, testified how one "old negro woman, who, after being subjected to the most brutal indecency from seven of the Yankees, was, at the proposition of one of them to 'finish the old Bitch,' put into a ditch and held under water until life was extinct. . . ."[27] In a letter that was discovered near Camden, South Carolina the day after Sherman's "bummers" passed through, Lieutenant Thomas J. Myers wrote the following words to his wife in Boston: "The damned niggers, as a general rule, prefer to stay at home, particularly after they found out that we only wanted the able-bodied men, (and, to tell you the truth, the youngest and best-looking women.) Sometimes

---

25. *Official Records*, Series I, Volume XVIII, page 464.

26. Rod Gragg (editor), *The Illustrated Confederate Reader* (New York: Gramercy Books, 1998), page 179.

27. Gragg, ibid., page 192.

we took off whole families and plantations of niggers, by way of repaying secessionists. But the useless part of them we soon manage to lose; sometimes in crossing rivers, sometimes in other ways."[28]

Dr. John Bachman, pastor of the Lutheran Church at Charleston, described the brutal treatment of the Negroes by the Northern invaders as follows:

> When Sherman's army came sweeping through Carolina, leaving a broad track of destruction for hundreds of miles, whose steps were accompanied with fire, and sword, and blood, reminding us of the tender mercies of the Duke of Alva, I happened to be at Cash's Depot, six miles from Cheraw. . . . A system of torture was practiced toward the weak, unarmed, and defenseless, which, as far as I know and believe, was universal throughout the whole course of that invading army. Before they arrived at a plantation, they inquired the names of the most faithful and trustworthy family servants; these were immediately seized, pistols were presented at their heads; with the most terrific curses, they were threatened to be shot if they did not assist them in finding buried treasures. If this did not succeed, they were tied up and cruelly beaten. Several poor creatures died under the infliction. The last resort was that

---

28. Letter dated February 26 1865; Henry Clay Dean, *Crimes of the Civil War and Curse of the Funding System* (Baltimore, Maryland: J. Wesley Smith and Brothers, 1869), pages 82-83. For a discussion of the authenticity of this letter, see George L. Christian, "Report of the Grand Camp, C. V., Department of Virginia, at Petersburg, Va., October 25, 1901; Robert Brock (editor), *Southern Historical Society Papers* (Richmond, Virginia: Southern Historical Society, 1901), Volume XXIX, pages 111-115.

of hanging, and the officers and men of the triumphant army of General Sherman were engaged in erecting gallows and hanging up these faithful and devoted servants. They were strung up until life was nearly extinct, when they were let down, suffered to rest awhile, then threatened and hung up again. It is not surprising that some should have been left hanging so long that they were taken down dead. Cooly and deliberately these hardened men proceeded on their way, as if they had perpetrated no crime, and as if the God of heaven would not pursue them with his vengeance. . . .

On Sunday, the negroes were dressed in their best suits. They were kicked, and knocked down and robbed of all their clothing, and they came to us in their shirtsleeves, having lost their hats, clothes, and shoes. Most of our own clothes had been hid in the woods. The negroes who had assisted in removing them were beaten and threatened with death, and compelled to show them where they were concealed. They cut open the trunks, threw my manuscripts and devotional books into a mud-hole, stole the ladies' jewelry, hair ornaments, etc., tore many garments into tatters, or gave the rest to the negro women to bribe them into criminal intercourse. These women afterward returned to us those articles that, after the mutilations, were scarcely worth preserving. The plantation, of one hundred and sixty negroes, was some distance from the house, and to this place successive parties of fifty at a time resorted for three long days and nights, the husbands and fathers being fired at and compelled to fly to the woods.[29]

---

29. "Vindication of Rev. Dr. John Bachman, of Charleston, S. C., in Answer to Rev. E. W. Hutter: in Regard to an Article Published in the 'Lutheran and Missionary,' of the 27th of July, 1865"; Gene Waddell (editor), *John Bachman: Selected Writings on Science, Race, and Religion*

Even more shocking is the following account given by William Gilmore Simms of Columbia:

> Something should be said in respect to the manner in which the negroes were treated by the Federals while in Columbia. . . . [The soldiers] were adverse to a connection with them; but few negroes were to be seen among them, and they were simply used as drudges, grooming horses, bearing burdens, humble of demeanor and rewarded with kicks, cuffs and curses, frequently without provocation. They despised and disliked the negro; openly professed their scorn or hatred, declared their unwillingness to have them as companions in arms or in company at all.
>
> Several instances have been given us of their modes of repelling the association of the negro, usually with blow of the fist, butt of the musket, slash of the sword or prick of the bayonet.
>
> Sherman himself looked on these things indifferently, if we are to reason from a single fact afforded us by Mayor Goodwyn. This gentleman, while walking with the general, heard the report of a gun. Both heard it, and immediately proceeded to the spot. There they found a group of soldiers, with a stalwart young negro fellow lying dead before them on the street, the body yet warm and bleeding. Pushing it with his feet, Sherman said, in his quick, hasty manner:
>
> "What does this mean, boys?"
>
> The reply was sufficiently cool and careless. "The d—d black rascal gave us his impudence, and we shot him."

(Athens, Georgia: University of Georgia Press, 2011), pages 307, 308, 310.

"Well, bury him at once! Get him out of sight!"

As they passed on, one of the party remarked:

"Is that the way, General, you treat such a case?"

"Oh!" said he, "we have no time now for courts martial and things of that sort!"

. . . The treatment of the negroes in their houses was, in the larger proportion of cases, quite as harsh as that which was shown to the whites. They were robbed in like manner, frequently of every article of clothing and provisions, and where the wigwam was not destroyed, it was effectually gutted. Few negroes having a good hat, good pair of shoes, good overcoat, but were incontinently deprived of them, and roughly handled when they remonstrated. . . .

The soldiers, in several cases which have been reported to us, pursued the slaves with the tenacity of blood-hounds; were at their elbows when they went forth, and hunted them up, at all hours, on the premises of the owner. Very frequent are instances where the negro, thus hotly pursued, besought protection of his master or mistress, sometimes voluntarily seeking a hiding place along the swamps of the river; at other times, finding it under the bed of the owner; and not leaving these places of refuge till long after the troops had departed.

For fully a month after they had gone, the negroes, singly or in squads, were daily making their way back to Columbia, having escaped from the Federals by dint of great perseverance and cunning, generally in wretched plight, half-starved and with little clothing. They represented the difficulties in the way of their escape to be very great, and the officers placing them finally under guards at night, and that they could only succeed in flight at the peril of life or limb. Many of these were negroes of Columbia, but the larger propor-

tion seemed to hail from Barnwell. They all sought pass-
ports to return to their owners and plantations.[30]

Even many honorable men in the North saw through
the thin philanthropic mask of the Abolitionist invasion of
the South. According to Rushmore G. Horton of New York,
"The driving off negroes from the plantations was no uncommon occurrence throughout the South. The negro is
naturally very much attached to his home, and when the
abolition officers came among them and told them they
were free to leave their masters and they did not do so,
they often became very angry with them, and *compelled*
them to enjoy what they called 'the blessings of freedom.'
These 'blessings,' it has been proved, consisted mainly of
'disease and death'" (emphasis in original).[31] It was estimated by Senator James R. Doolittle of Wisconsin, himself
an ardent Abolitionist, that one million Negroes had per-
ished from disease, neglect, and other factors associated
with the invasion of the South and a disruption of its institutions.[32] According to Robert L. Dabney's October 21, 1865
letter to Major-General Oliver O. Howard, half the Black
population of Louisiana were lying in their graves by the
end of the war.[33]

---

30. William Gilmore Simms, *The Sack and Destruction of Columbia, South Carolina* (Columbia, South Carolina: Power Press of the Daily Phoenix, 1865), pages 60-62.

31. Horton, *History of the Great Civil War*, pages 291-292.

32. Speech at New Haven, Connecticut; *Appleton's Annual Cyclopedia and Register of Important Events of the Year 1865* (New York: D. Appleton and Company, 1866), Volume V, page 810.

33. Robert Lewis Dabney, *Discussions* (Mexico, Missouri: S. B. Ervin, 1897), Volume IV, page 38.

Such accounts, which would literally fill volumes and sicken the soul of any civilized man or woman, are rarely brought to light by those who propagate the myth that the war was fought by the Northern armies with the welfare of the Black race in mind. We will conclude with the following words of Dennis A. Mahony, editor of the *Dubuque Herald*, written in the Old Capitol Prison at Washington, D. C., where he was imprisoned in 1862 by the Lincoln Administration for his Democratic sentiments. In his journal entry for the ninth of September, Mahoney recorded the entrance into the prison of several Confederate prisoners of war, captured at the battle of Fredericksburg, Virginia:

> Several prisoners have been brought here today from the neighborhood of Fredericksburgh. Among them were some negroes, one of them, a large, intelligent spoken fellow, was very anxious to see his master, who, having been paroled, was not brought to the prison. I asked this slave whether he would go back to his master.
>
> "Yes, sir," said he, "I don't want to stay here; my master always treated me well, and I don't want to leave him."
>
> "But," said I, "they will keep you here, or send you north."
>
> "Well, massa," said he, "if they won't let me go home, I can't help it; but, if they will let me away, I will go with my master."
>
> In connection with this, I may say, from conversations I have had with nearly every one of the male contrabands around the premises, that every one of them desires, and designs, if he should have an opportu-

nity, to go back to his master. Most of them were brought here against their will, and, if left free to choose, they will go back to their old masters, in preference to remaining here or going north.[34]

Further comment on the "freedom" given to the Southern Blacks by the Northern invaders is not necessary.

---

34. Dennis A. Mahony, *Prisoner of State* (New York: G. W. Carleton and Company, 1863), pages 235-236.

APPENDIX FOUR

Republican Quotes on the Negro

It is not the cause of the negro, but that of the . . . white man that is involved in this question [of the Territories].[1]

When southern people tell us they are no more responsible for the origin of slavery, than we; I acknowledge the fact. When it is said that the institution exists; and that it is very difficult to get rid of it, in any satisfactory way, I can understand and appreciate the saying. I surely will not blame them for not doing what I should not know how to do myself. If all earthly power were given me, I should not know what to do, as to the existing institution. My first impulse would be to free all the slaves, and send them to Liberia, — to their own native land. But a moment's reflection would convince me, that whatever of high hope, (as I think there is) there may be in this, in the long run, its sudden execution is impossible. If they were all landed there in a day, they would

---

1. Gideon Welles; *Hartford Evening News*, 1854; Warshauer, *Connecticut in the American Civil War*, page 39.

all perish in the next ten days; and there are not surplus shipping and surplus money enough in the world to carry them there in many times ten days. What then? Free them all, and keep them among us as underlings? Is it quite certain that this betters their condition? I think I would not hold one in slavery, at any rate; yet the point is not clear enough for me to denounce people upon. What next? Free them, and make them politically and socially, our equals? My own feelings will not admit of this; and if mine would, we well know that those of the great mass of white people will not. Whether this feeling accords with justice and sound judgment, is not the sole question, if indeed, it is any part of it. A universal feeling, whether well or ill founded, can not be safely disregarded. We can not, then, make them equals. . . .

Let it not be said I am contending for the establishment of political and social equality between the whites and blacks. I have already said the contrary.[2]

Our aim should be to Americanize this country . . . and keep the colored race within its present limits. This is the white man's party; it is not because we feel any burning zeal in the black man's cause, that we resist the progress of Slavery in this country. We like the white man better than we do the black. We believe the Caucasian variety of the human species, superior to the Negro variety. . . . Color is not the trouble; thick lips and wooly hair are not the objections. It is, that the Caucasian variety is intrinsically a better breed, of better brain, of better moral traits, better capacity in every way, than the Ne-

2. Abraham Lincoln, Peoria, Illinois, October 15, 1854; Basler, *Collected Works of Lincoln*, Volume II, pages 255-256, 267.

gro, or the Mongolian, or the Malay, or the Red American.

The Republicans mean to preserve all of this country that they can, from the pestilential presence of the black man. Some people think themselves witty and smart, in calling this cause the Black Republican cause; to our minds it is intrinsically aristocratic; it aims to save the country for the white man, and is aristocratic because it impliedly avows a preference of the white race, as settlers, over the black race.[3]

[The Democrats] of the South live among niggers, work among niggers, eat among niggers, drink among niggers and sleep with niggers. . . . [T]hey never get out of sight of a nigger, and their constant intercourse with niggers corrupts even their manners and language, and leads them to acquire nigger antics, nigger pronunciation, and nigger language. . . . The Anti-Nebraska men are laboring to keep Kansas and her white people free from the foul contamination with niggers; their purpose is to keep niggers out of Kansas.[4]

It is not negro equality only, but negro government, negro supremacy, and negro rights to the exclusion and abasement of White Men, that the Republican party oppose. Nigger! Nigger!! What would Mr. Buchanan's people do without the eternal inevitable nigger.[5]

3. Thomas M. Day, *The Courant* (Hartford, Connecticut), March 6, 1856.

4. *The Free Press* (Pittsfield, Illinois), July 31, 1856.

5. Michael Garber, *Daily Evening Courier* (Madison, Indiana), August 26, 1856.

A separation of the races is the only perfect preventive of amalgamation; but as immediate separation is impossible, the next best thing is to keep them apart where they are not already together. If white and black people never get together in Kansas, they will never mix blood in Kansas.[6]

No slaveholders and no niggers in the territories — white men must own and forever occupy the great west. Nigger slaves shall not be allowed to work among, associate, or amalgamate with white people. Democrats must go to the old slave states if they want to own and live among niggers. These are Republican ideas . . . against the progress of Negro slavery, Negro amalgamation, Negro association, and every other infernal Negro business.[7]

The Republican party had uniformly and most emphatically repudiated the idea that they had anything whatever to do with negroes or negro rights . . . and declared, always and everywhere, that they aimed at the good of the white men of the country, and had nothing to do with negroes. . . .[8]

The "negro question," as we understand it, is a white man's question, the question of the right of free white laborers to the soil of the territories. It is not to be

6. Lincoln, Springfield, Illinois, June 26, 1857; Basler, *Collected Works of Lincoln*, Volume II, page 408.

7. Joseph Cover, *Grant County Herald* (Wisconsin), October 24, 1857.

8. *New York Times* editorial, 1858; Kenneth M. Stampp, *The Imperiled Union: Essays on the Background of the Civil War* (New York: Oxford University Press 1980), page 109.

crushed or retarded by shouting "Sambo" at us. We have no Sambo in our platform. . . . We object to Sambo. We don't want him about. We insist that he shall not be forced upon us.[9]

[The Republican party is not] a nigger-worshipping, equality-advocating organization.
    . . . I am resolutely opposed to the "equalizing of the races" and it no more necessarily follows that we should fellowship with negroes because our policy strikes off their shackles, than it would to take felons to our embraces, because we might remonstrate against cruelty to them in our penitentiaries.
    . . . [Y]ou may always find the Journal opposing the policy of "putting too much nigger in our platform."[10]

The industry, virtue and patriotism of the free white laboring classes is the great bulwark of our political freedom. Our cause is that of the white man, and our object the encouragement and prosperity of free white labor, and the spread of free society.[11]

My declarations upon this subject of negro slavery may be misrepresented, but cannot be misunderstood. I have said that I do not understand the Declaration [of

---

9. John Greiner, *Columbus Gazette* (Ohio), 1858; Earl B. Wiley, "'Governor' John Greiner and Chase's Bid for the Presidency in 1860," *Ohio State Archaeological and Historical Quarterly*, Number LVIII (1940), pages 261-262.

10. Charles L. Wilson to Lyman Trumbull, Chicago, Illinois, May 12, 1858; Mark Hubbard (editor), *Illinois's War: The Civil War in Documents* (Athens, Ohio: Ohio University Press, 2013), page 39.

11. *Illinois State Chronicle* (Decatur), June 17, 1858.

Independence] to mean that all men were created equal in all respects. . . . Certainly the negro is not our equal in color – perhaps not in many other respects. . . .[12]

We are opposed to negro equality and to all who favor negro equality, and to those who seek its accomplishment, by compelling white men to work side by side with negro slaves.[13]

I, for one, am very much disposed to favor the colonization of such free negroes as are willing to go in Central America. I want to have nothing to do either with the free negro or the slave negro. We, the Republican party, are the white man's party. We are for free white men, and for making white labor respectable and honorable, which it never can be when negro slave labor is brought into competition with it. We wish to settle the Territories with free white men, and we are willing that this negro race should go anywhere that it can to better its condition, wishing them God speed wherever they go. We believe it is better for us that they should not be among us. I believe it will be better for them to go elsewhere.[14]

. . . [T]his is the true complexion of all I have ever said in regard to the institution of slavery and the black race. This is the whole of it, and anything that argues me into his idea of perfect social and political equality

12. Lincoln, July 17, 1858, Springfield, Illinois; Basler, *Collected Works of Lincoln*, Volume II, page 520.

13. *Chicago Weekly Times*, July 22, 1858.

14. Lyman Trumbull, Chicago, Illinois, August 7, 1858; *Speech of Hon. Lyman Trumbull*, page 13.

with the negro, is but a specious and fantastic arrange-
ment of words, by which a man can prove a horse chestnut to be a chestnut horse. I will say here, while upon
this subject, that I have no purpose directly or indirectly
to interfere with the institution of slavery in the States
where it exists. I believe I have no lawful right to do so,
and I have no inclination to do so. I have no purpose to
introduce political and social equality between the
white and the black races. There is a physical difference
between the two, which in my judgment will probably
forever forbid their living together upon the footing of
perfect equality, and inasmuch as it becomes a necessity
that there must be a difference, I, as well as Judge
Douglas, am in favor of the race to which I belong, having the superior position. I have never said anything to
the contrary.[15]

While I was at the hotel to-day an elderly gentleman
called upon me to know whether I was really in favor of
producing a perfect equality between the negroes and
white people. While I had not proposed to myself on this
occasion to say much on that subject, yet as the question
was asked me I thought I would occupy perhaps five
minutes in saying something in regard to it. I will say
then that I am not, nor ever have been in favor of bringing
about in any way the social and political equality of the
white and black races – that I am not nor ever have been
in favor of making voters or jurors of negroes, nor of
qualifying them to hold office, nor to intermarry with
white people; and I will say in addition to this that there
is a physical difference between the white and black races

---

15. Lincoln, Ottawa, Illinois, August 21, 1858; Basler, *Collected Works
of Lincoln*, Volume III, page 16.

which I believe will forever forbid the two races living together on terms of social and political equality. And inasmuch as they cannot so live, while they do remain together there must be the position of the superior and the inferior, and I as much as any other man am in favor of having the superior position assigned to the white race. . . .

I tell [Judge Douglas] very frankly that I am not in favor of negro citizenship. . . . Now my opinion is that the different States have the power to make a negro a citizen under the Constitution of the United States if they choose. . . . If the State of Illinois had that power I should be opposed to the exercise of it. That is all I have to say about it.[16]

Now irrespective of the moral aspect of this question as to whether there is a right or wrong in enslaving a negro, I am still in favor of our new Territories being in such a condition that white men may find a home . . . where they can settle upon new soil and better their condition in life. I am in favor of this not merely . . . for our own people who are born amongst us, but as an outlet for free white people everywhere, the world over. . . .[17]

I do not perceive how I can express myself more plainly than I have done in the foregoing extracts. In four of them I have expressly disclaimed all intention to bring about social and political equality between the white and black races, and, in all the rest, I have done

16. Lincoln, September 18, 1858, Charleston, Illinois; Basler, ibid., pages 145-146, 179.

17. Lincoln, Alton, Illinois, October 15, 1858; Basler, ibid., page 312.

the same thing by clear implication.[18]

[With the Democrats] it is niggers, niggers, niggers, first and always . . . . Tariff and everything else must be made to suit their niggers. Our interest . . . is the White man's interest. I am proud to say that I belong to the white man's party.[19]

It was asked whether we would be in favor, in the northern States, of receiving the negro immigration from the South? I would that there was not a negro upon this whole continent; and that they are here has been a monstrous wrong, from the first to the last. . . . The Republican party does not anywhere contend that negroes should have the right of suffrage. They do not insist that negroes should be our equals in association. They merely ask, as a matter of sheer justice, that their humanity shall be recognized — that they shall have the right to go into the courts and redress their wrongs. . . . Gentlemen must see that there is a vast difference between conceding equal political and social rights to the negro, and yielding to him the common rights of humanity.[20]

Negro equality. Fudge!! How long in the Government of a God great enough to make and maintain this universe, shall there continue to be knaves to vend and

18. Lincoln, letter to James Brown, October 18, 1858; Basler, ibid., page 399.

19. Alfred Caldwell, speech in Richmond on February 7, 1859; Patricia P. Hicken, "Antislavery in Virginia, 1831-1861" (Ph.D. dissertation, University of Virginia, 1968), page 723.

20. Representative Clark B. Cochrane of New York; *Congressional Globe*, Thirty-Fifth Congress, Second Session, February 11, 1859, page 918.

fools to gulp, so low a piece of demagoguism as this?[21]

We are thus free to contemplate without prejudice the legitimate effects that would flow from the adoption of the policy of the Republican or of the Democratic party, and to decide into whose hands we shall intrust the reins of government. The decision of this question will determine by what race of men the unoccupied territories shall be peopled.

The policy of the Republican party invites the Anglo-Saxon, the Celt, the Gaul, and others of Caucasian blood, by its proposed preemption and homestead laws, to enter and occupy them, and by the exclusion of slavery it will practically exclude the negro and kindred races.[22]

The Republican party contemplates primarily the interest of Free White Labor, for which it struggles to secure the unoccupied territory of the Union.[23]

The people of the North will never consent to come in contact with the institution of slavery in the territories. To work side by side with negro slaves . . . will leave [them in a] condition little above slaves themselves. Let [Southerners] keep their niggers if they will, but they must not bring them in contact with us. No

---

21. Lincoln, speech notes, September, 1859; Basler, *Collected Works of Lincoln*, Volume III, page 328.

22. Iowa Senator James Harlan, *Congressional Globe*, Thirty-Sixth Congress, First Session, January 4, 1860, page 55.

23. Horace Greeley, *Twenty-Eight Annual Report of the American Anti-Slavery Society, by the Executive Committee For the Year Ending May 1, 1861* (New York: American Anti-Slavery Society, 1861), page 32.

matter whether we are opposed to the extension of slavery from love of humanity and justice, or from hatred of niggers (of the latter class are many Illinois Republicans) we are terribly in earnest in our opposition to the extension of that institution.[24]

We make no pretensions to special interest in or liking for the African Race. . . . [W]e maintain the right of every man to himself and his own limbs and muscles . . . but we do not like negroes, and heartily wish no individual of that race had ever been brought to America. We hope the day will come when the whole negro race in this country, being fully at liberty, will gradually, peacefully, freely draw off and form a community by themselves somewhere near the Equator, or join their brethren in lineage in Africa or the West Indies.[25]

[We protest] the silly lie that ours is a "negro party" – that "it has no idea but "nigger! nigger!" – that it cares nothing or thinks nothing of the interests and welfare of White Men.[26]

The negro is a fellowbeing, and entitled to be treated as such [but] at the same time [we] tell him that socially he cannot be the equal of the white, for the line drawn between the two by the Creator is too strongly marked to be overlooked.[27]

There are men in the Northern States who uphold

24. Stampp, *Imperilled Union*, pages 109-110.

25. *New York Tribune*, February 29, 1860.

26. Ibid., March 6, 1860.

27. *New York Courier and Enquirer*, July 13, 1860.

and advocate that doctrine [of Negro equality], — but they are few in number and are not increasing. The Republican party, as such, has never been committed to it. . . .

The field for carrying this principle into effect is in State legislation. Yet in how many of those States in which the Republicans have full political sway, have negroes been placed on a footing of complete political equality with whites?

. . . Before anything can be done by the North for Southern slaves, they must be set free, — and then they fall at once into the category of "free negroes" whom the North . . . absolutely and thoroughly despise. Pray how is the doctrine of negro equality to be "forced upon the South" by the Republicans, when they scout and scorn it for the free negroes of the North?

In point of fact, the Republicans . . . entertain very much the same feeling towards the negroes as other sensible white men, North and South. . . . They recognize their degradation — their mental, social and political inferiority to the whites, as a fact . . . and they have not the slightest disposition to give them authority or control over social movements or the development of social civilization. It is a great mistake, moreover, to suppose that as a party the Republicans are in favor of emancipating the slaves. . . .

We fear, indeed, that our Southern brethren over-rate the philanthropy of the Republicans towards the negroes. . . . We do not believe they have any more love of the negro . . . than the rest of mankind, North and South. Whenever the matter comes to be practically tested, we presume it will be discovered to be pretty thoroughly a white man's party . . . looking mainly and steadily to the advancement of the interests, the development of the character and the promotion of the welfare and happiness of the great mass of our white American society. So far as their apprehensions that the Republicans will introduce an era of negro equality are real, our Southern friends may dismiss them at once.[28]

How natural has it been to assume that the motive of those who have protested against the extension of slavery, was an unnatural sympathy with the negro instead of what it always has really been, concern for the welfare of the white man. . . .

The great fact is now fully realized that the African race here is a foreign and feeble element, like the Indians, incapable of assimilation, . . . and that it is a pitiful exotic, unwisely and unnecessarily transplanted into our fields, and which it is unprofitable to cultivate at the cost of the desolation of the native vineyard.[29]

. . . [It has been] said that we Black Republicans were advocates of negro equality, and that we wanted to build up a black government. Sir, it will be one of the most blessed ideas of the times, if it shall come to this, that we will make inducements to every free black among us to find his home in a more congenial climate in Central America or Lower Mexico, and we will be divested of every one of them. . . .[30]

The truth is, the nigger is an unpopular institution

---

28. *New York Times*, August 28, 1860, page 4.

29. William H. Seward, Albany, New York, September 4, 1860; *Speeches of William H. Seward*, pages 5, 6.

30. Benjamin F. Wade, *Congressional Globe*, Thirty-Sixth Congress, Second Session, December 17, 1860, page 104.

in the free States. Even those who are unwilling to rob them of all the rights of humanity, and are willing to let them have a spot on earth on which to live and to labor and to enjoy the fruits of their toil, do not care to be brought into close contact with them.[31]

In the State where I live, we do not like negroes. We do not disguise our dislike.[32]

Our republican system was meant for a homogeneous people. As long as the Negroes continue to live with the whites they will constitute a threat to the national life. Family life might also collapse and the increase of "the mixed breed bastards," might some day challenge the supremacy of the white man.[33]

Why . . . should people of your race be colonized, and where? Why should they leave this country? This is, perhaps, the first question for proper consideration. You and we are different races. We have between us a broader difference than exists between almost any other two races. Whether it is right or wrong I need not discuss, but this physical difference is a great disadvantage to us both, as I think your race suffers very greatly, many of them, by living among us, while ours suffers from your presence. In a word we suffer on each side. If this be admitted, it affords a reason at least why we should be separated.

---

31. *Illinois State Journal* (Springfield), March 22, 1862.

32. John Sherman, *Congressional Globe*, Thirty-Seventh Congress, Second Session, April 2, 1862, page 1491.

33. James Mitchell, May 15, 1862; Basler, *Abraham Lincoln Quarterly*, Volume VI, Number 3, page 172.

You are freemen I suppose. Perhaps you have long been free, or all your lives. Your race is suffering, in my judgment, the greatest wrong inflicted on any people. But even when you cease to be slaves, you are yet far removed from being placed on an equality with the white race. You are cut off from many of the advantages which the other race enjoys. . . . The aspiration of men is to enjoy equality with the best when free, but on this broad continent, not a single man of your race is made the equal of a single man of ours. Go where you are treated the best, and the ban is still upon you. I believe in its [slavery's] general evil effects on the white race. See our present condition – the country engaged in war – and then consider what we know to be the truth. But for your race among us there could not be war, although many men engaged on either side do not care for you one way or the other. . . . It is better for us both therefore to be separated. . . .[34]

I don't see why we can't have some sense about negroes. . . . I like niggers well enough as niggers, but when fools and idiots try and make niggers better than ourselves, I have an opinion.[35]

Iron is iron and steel is steel; and all the popular clamor on earth will not impart to one the qualities of the other. So a nigger is not a white man, and all the Psalm

34. Lincoln, statement to a Black delegation at the White House, August 14, 1862; Basler, *Collected Works of Lincoln*, Volume V, pages 371-372.

35. William T. Sherman, letter to his wife, September 8, 1864; Brooks D. Simpson and Jean V. Berlin (editors), *Sherman's Civil War: Selected Correspondence of William T. Sherman, 1860-1865* (Chapel Hill, North Carolina: University of North Carolina Press, 1999), page 727.

singing on earth won't make him so.[36]

> I can hardly believe that the South and North can live in peace, unless we can get rid of the negroes. Certainly they cannot if we don't get rid of the negroes whom we have armed and disciplined and who have fought with us. . . . I believe that it would be better to export them all to some fertile country with a good climate, which they came have to themselves.[37]

---

36. Sherman, letter to J. A. R., September 12, 1864; Henry B. Dawson (editor), *The Historical Magazine and Notes and Queries Concerning the Antiquities, History and Biography of America* (Morisania, New York: Henry B. Dawson, 1872), Volume I, Third Series, page 113.

37. Lincoln, April 11, 1865; *Butler's Book*, Volume II, page 903.

BIBLIOGRAPHY

— *Appleton's Annual Cyclopedia and Register of Important Events of the Year 1865* (New York: D. Appleton and Company, 1866).

— *Herkimer Convention, The Voice of New York: Proceedings of the Herkimer Mass Convention of Oct. 26, 1847* (*Albany Atlas Extra*, November 1847).

— *Journal of the Constitutional Convention of the State of Illinois* (Springfield: C.H. Lanphier, 1862).

— *Journal of the House of Representatives of the State of Indiana During the Thirty-Fifth Session of the General Assembly* (Indianapolis, Indiana: J.P. Chapman, 1851).

— *Official Records of the War of the Rebellion* (seventy volumes; Washington, D.C.: Government Printing Office, 1894).

— *Report of the Debates and Proceedings of the Convention for the Revision of the Constitution of the State of Indiana, 1850* (two volumes; Indianapolis, Indiana: A.H. Brown, 1850).

— *Report to the Primary School Committee, June 15, 1846, on the Petition of Sundry Colored Persons, for the Abolition of the Schools for Colored Children, With the City Solicitor's Opinion* (Boston: J.H. Eastburn, 1846).

— *The Revised Laws of Indiana* (Indianapolis, Indiana: Douglass and Maguire, 1831).

— *The Revised Laws of Illinois* (Vandalia, Illinois: Greiner and Sherman, 1833).

Anthrop, Mary, "Indiana Emigrants to Liberia," *The Indiana Historian*, March 2000.

Barker, Charles Albro (editor), *Memoirs of Elisha Oliver Crosby: Reminiscences of California and Guatemala From 1849 to 1864* (San Marino, California: Huntington Library, 1945).

Basler, Roy (editor), *Abraham Lincoln: His Speeches and Writings* (Cleveland, Ohio: The World Publishing Company, 1946).

Basler, Roy (editor), *The Collected Works of Abraham Lincoln* (eight volumes; New Brunswick, New Jersey: Rutgers University Press, 1953).

Beale, Howard K. (editor), *The Diary of Edward Bates*, 1859-1866 (Washington, D.C.: Government Printing Office, 1933).

Bellows, Donald, "A Study of British Conservative Reaction to the American Civil War," *The Journal of Southern History*, Volume LI, Number 4 (November, 1985).

Bennett, Lerone, Jr., *Forced Into Glory: Abraham Lincoln's White Dream* (Chicago, Illinois: Johnson Publishing Company, Inc., 2000).

Berlin, Ira, et. al (editors), *Free at Last: A Documentary History of Slavery, Freedom, and the Civil War* (New York: The New Press, 1992).

Bigelow, John, *Retrospections of an Active Life* (three volumes; New York: The Baker and Taylor Company, 1909).

Burlingame, Michael and Turner, John R. (editors), *Inside Lincoln's White House: The Complete Civil War Diary of John Hay* (Carbondale, Illinois: Southern Illinois University Press, 1997).

Burlingame, Michael, *Abraham Lincoln: A Life* (two volumes; Baltimore: Johns Hopkins University Press, 2008).

Burnet, Jacob, *Notes on the Early Settlement of the North-Western Territory* (Cincinnati, Ohio: Derby, Bradley and Company, 1847).

Burrows, Edwin G. and Wallace, Mike, *Gotham: a History of New York City to 1898* (New York: Oxford University Press, 1998).

Butler, Benjamin F., *Butler's Book* (two volumes; Boston: A. M. Thayer and Company, 1892).

Carey, Matthew, Jr. (pseudonym), *The Democratic Speaker's Hand Book* (Cincinnati, Ohio: Miami Print and Publishing Company, 1868).

Carpenter, Francis B., *The Inner Life of Abraham Lincoln: Six Months at the White House* (New York: Hurd and Houghton, 1867).

Carpenter, Stephen D., *The Logic of History: Five Hundred Political Texts Being Concentrated Extracts of Abolitionism* (Madison, Wisconsin: self-published, 1864).

Chace, Elizabeth Buffum and Lovell, Lucy Buffum, *Two Quaker Sisters* (New York, Liveright Publishing Corporation, 1937).

Chadwick, French Ensor, *Causes of the Civil War* (New York: Harper and Brothers Publishers, 1906).

Chittenden, Lucius E., *Recollections of President Lincoln and His Administration* (New York: Harper and Brothers, 1891).

Cole, Arthur Charles (editor), *The Constitutional Debates of 1847* (Springfield, Illinois: Illinois State Historical Library, 1919).

Christian, George L., "Report of the Grand Camp, C.V., Department of Virginia, at Petersburg, Va., October 25, 1901;

Robert Brock (editor), *Southern Historical Society Papers* (Richmond, Virginia: Southern Historical Society, 1901), Volume XXIX.

Cole, Arthur Charles, *The Centennial History of Illinois: The Era of the Civil War, 1848-1870* (Springfield: Illinois Centennial Commission, 1919).

Crofts, Daniel W., *Lincoln and the Politics of Slavery: The Other Thirteenth Amendment and the Struggle to Save the Union* (Chapel Hill, North Carolina, University of North Carolina Press, 2016).

Curtis, Benjamin Robbins, *Executive Power* (Boston: Little, Brown and Company, 1862).

Dabney, Robert Lewis, *Discussions: Secular* (Mexico, Missouri: S.B. Ervin, 1897).

Davis, Jefferson, *The Rise and Fall of the Confederate Government* (two volumes; New York: D. Appleton and Company, 1881).

Dawson, Henry B. (editor), *The Historical Magazine and Notes and Queries Concerning the Antiquities, History and Biography of America* (Morisania, New York: Henry B. Dawson, 1872).

Dean, Henry Clay, *Crimes of the Civil War and Curse of the Funding System* (Baltimore, Maryland: J. Wesley Smith and Brothers, 1869).

Delany, Martin Robinson, *The Condition, Elevation, Emigration, and Destiny of the Colored People of the United States* (Philadelphia: self-published, 1852).

Douglass, Frederick, *The Life and Times of Frederick Douglass* (London: Christian Age Office, 1882).

Duncan, John M., *Travels Through Part of the United States and Canada in 1818 and 1819* (two volumes; New York: W.B. Gilley, 1823).

Fleming, Walter L. (editor), *General W. T. Sherman as College President: A Collection of Letters, Documents, and Other Material Chiefly From Private Sources, Relating to the Life and Activities of General William Tecumseh Sherman* (Cleveland, Ohio: The Arthur H. Clark Company, 1912).

Foner, Philip S. (editor), *The Life and Writings of Frederick Douglass* (five volumes; New York: International Publishers, 1950).

Foner, Eric, *The Fiery Trial: Abraham Lincoln and American Slavery* (New York: W.W. Norton and Company, 2010).

Fredrickson, George M., "A Man But Not a Brother: Abraham Lincoln and Racial Equality," *The Journal of Southern History*, Volume XLI, Number 1 (February, 1975).

Frothingham, Octavius Brooks, *Theodore Parker: A Biography* (Boston: Osgood, 1874).

Garrison, Wendell Phillips and Garrison, Francis Jackson, *William Lloyd Garrison, 1805-1870* (Boston: Houghton, Mifflin Company, 1894).

Goodwin, Doris Kearns, *Team of Rivals: The Political Genius of Abraham Lincoln* (New York: Simon and Schuster, 2005).

Gragg, Rod (editor), *The Illustrated Confederate Reader* (New York: Gramercy Books, 1998).

Greeley, Horace, *Twenty-Eight Annual Report of the American Anti-Slavery Society, by the Executive Committee For the Year Ending May 1, 1861* (New York: American Anti-Slavery Society, 1861).

Horton, Rushmore G., *A Youth's History of the Great Civil War of the United States From 1861 to 1865* (New York: Van Evrie, Horton and Company, 1868).

Hamilton, Thomas, *Men and Manners in America* (Edinburgh, Scotland: William Blackwood, 1833).

Harris, N. Dwight, *History of Negro Servitude in Illinois* (Chicago: A.C. McClurg and Company, 1904).

Harrison, Lowell H., *Lincoln of Kentucky* (Lexington, Kentucky: University Press of Kentucky, 2000).

Helper, Hinton Rowan, *The Impending Crisis of the South: How To Meet It* (New York: A.B. Burdick, Publishers, 1857).

Helper, Hinton Rowan, *Black Negroes in Negroland* (New York: Carleton, 1868).

Herr, Pamela and Spence, Mary Lee (editors), *Letters of Jessie Benton Frémont* (Chicago: University of Illinois Press, 1993).

Hicken, Patricia P., "Antislavery in Virginia, 1831-1861" (Ph.D. dissertation, University of Virginia, 1968).

Hopkins, James F. (editor), *The Papers of Henry Clay: The Rising Statesman 1815-1820* (three volumes; Lexington, Kentucky: University of Kentucky Press, 1961).

Howard, Victor B., *Religion and the Radical Republican Movement, 1860-1870* (Lexington, Kentucky: University Press of Kentucky, 1986).

Hubbard, Mark (editor), *Illinois's War: The Civil War in Documents* (Athens, Ohio: Ohio University Press, 2013).

Hume, John F., *The Abolitionists, Together With Personal Memories of the Struggle For Human Rights* (New York: G. P. Putnam's Sons, 1905).

Hurd, John C., *The Law of Freedom and Bondage in the United States* (two volumes; Boston: Little, Brown and Company, 1858).

Johannsen, Robert W., *Lincoln, the South, and Slavery* (Baton Rouge: Louisiana State University Press, 1991).

Kelley, William D., *Lincoln and Stanton* (New York: G. P. Putnam's Sons, 1885).

Kennedy, W. Sloane, *John Greenleaf Whittier: His Life, Genius, and Writings* (Boston: D. Lothrop, 1886).

Krum, John M., "The Death of Elijah P. Lovejoy: A Voice From the Past," *Journal of the Illinois State Historical Society*, Volume IV, January 1, 1912.

Lamon, Ward Hill, *The Life of Abraham Lincoln: From His Birth to His Inauguration as President* (Boston: James R. Osgood and Company, 1872).

Leland, Charles Godfrey, *Abraham Lincoln* (New York: G.P. Putnam's Sons, 1881).

Lester, Charles Edward, *Life and Public Services of Charles Sumner* (New York: United States Publishing Company, 1874).

Litwack, Leon F., *North of Slavery: The Negro in the Free States, 1790-1860* (Chicago, Illinois: University of Chicago Press, 1961).

Lupton, John A., "Abraham Lincoln and the Corwin Amendment," *Illinois Heritage* (September-October 2006), Volume IX, Number 5.

Lusk, David W., *Politics and Politicians: A Succinct History of the Politics of Illinois From 1856 to 1884* (Springfield, Illinois: H.W. Rokker, 1887).

Luthin, Reinhard H., "Abraham Lincoln and the Tariff," *The American Historical Review* (July, 1944), Volume XLIX, Number 4.

Magness, Phillip W. and Page, Sebastian N., *Colonization After Emancipation: Lincoln and the Movement for Black Resettlement* (Columbia, Missouri: University of Missouri Press, 2011).

Mahony, Dennis A., *Prisoner of State* (New York: G. W. Carleton and Company, 1863).

May, Samuel Joseph, *Some Recollections of Our Antislavery Conflict* (Boston: Fields, Osgood and Company, 1869).

McPherson, Edward, *The Political History of the United States of America, During the Great Rebellion* (Washington, D. C.: Philip and Solomons, 1865).

McPherson, James M., *The Negro's Civil War: How American Blacks Felt and Acted During the War For the Union* (New York: Vintage Civil War Library, 2003).

Meites, Jerome B., "The 1847 Illinois Constitutional Convention and Persons of Color," *Journal of the Illinois State Historical Society*, Volume CVIII, Number 3-4 (Fall/Winter 2015).

Merrill, Walter M. (editor), *The Letters of William Lloyd Garrison* (six volumes; Cambridge: Harvard University Press, 1981).

Miller, Marion Mills and Carpenter, Francis Bicknell (editors), *The Works of Abraham Lincoln: Speeches and Debates, 1858-1859* (New York: C. S. Hammond and Company, 1907).

Moore, Frank (editor), *The Rebellion Record: A Diary of American Events* (seven volumes; New York: G. P. Putnam, 1864).

Munford, Beverley B., *Virginia's Attitude Toward Slavery and Secession* (New York: Longmans, Green and Company, 1909).

Nation, Richard F., "Violence and the Rights of African Americans in Civil War-Era Indiana: The Case of James Hays," *Indiana Magazine of History*, Volume C, Number 3 (September 2004).

Nevins, Allan, *Frémont: Pathmarker of the West* (Lincoln, Nebraska: University of Nebraska Press, 1992).

Nicolay, John G. and Hay, John (editors), *Abraham Lincoln: Complete Works, Comprising His Speeches, Letters, State Papers, and Miscellaneous Writings* (New York: The Century Company, 1894).

Nicolay, John G. and Hay, John, *Abraham Lincoln: A History* (ten volumes; New York: The Century Company, 1914).

Niven, John (editor), *The Salmon P. Chase Papers* (five volumes; Kent, Ohio: Kent State University Press, 1993).

Oates, Stephen B., *Builders of the Dream: Abraham Lincoln and Martin Luther King, Jr.* (Fort Wayne, Indiana: Lincoln Library and Museum, 1982).

Parker, Joel, "The Character of the Rebellion and the Conduct of the War," *North American Review* (Cambridge: Welch, Bigelow, and Company, 1862), October 1862.

Parker, Theodore, *John Brown's Expedition Reviewed in a Letter from Rev. Theodore Parker, at Rome, to Francis Jackson, Boston* (Boston: The Fraternity, 1860).

Pease, Theodore Calvin, *The Frontier State, 1818-1848* (Chicago: A. C. McClurg & Company, 1919).

Phillips, Wendell, *The Constitution a Pro-Slavery Compact* (New York: American Anti-Slavery Society, 1856).

Phillips, Wendell, *Speeches, Lectures, and Letters by Wendell Phillips* (Boston: Lee and Shepard, 1894).

Piatt, Donn, *Memories of the Men Who Saved the Union* (New York: Belford, Clarke and Company, 1887).

Quarles, Benjamin A., *Lincoln and the Negro* (New York: Oxford University Press, 1962).

Rael, Patrick, *Eighty-Eight Years: The Long Death of Slavery in the United States, 1777-1865* (Athens, Geor-gia: University of Georgia Press, 2015).

Randall, James G., *The Civil War and Reconstruction* (Boston: D. C. Heath and Company, 1937).

Rawley, James A., *Race and Politics: "Bleeding Kansas" and the Coming of the Civil War* (Lincoln, Nebraska: University of Nebraska Press, 1979).

Raymond, Henry J. (editor), *The Life and Public Services of Abraham Lincoln, Together With His State Papers* (New York: Derby and Miller, 1865).

Rhodes, James Ford, *History of the United States from the Compromise of 1850: 1860-1862* (seven volumes: New York: The Macmillan Company, 1893-1906).

Richardson, James D., *A Compilation of the Messages and Papers of the Presidents* (eight volumes; Washington D. C.: Bureau of National Literature, 1897).

Riley, Benjamin Franklin, *The White Man's Burden: A Discussion of the Interracial Question With Special Reference to the Responsibility of the White Race to the Negro Problem* (Birmingham, Alabama: Self-Published, 1910).

Ripley, C. Peter (editor), *The Black Abolitionist Papers* (five volumes; Chapel Hill, North Carolina: University of North Carolina Press, 1985-1992).

Rutherford, Mildred Lewis, *Truths of History* (Athens, Georgia: self-published, 1920).

Scheips, Paul J., "Lincoln and the Chiriqui Colonization Project," *The Journal of Negro History*, Volume XXXVII, Number 4 (October, 1952).

Seilhamer, George O., *History of the Republican Party: Narrative and Critical History, 1856-1898* (two volumes; New York: Judge Publishing Company, 1899).

Seward, William H., *Speeches of William H. Seward: Lincoln Campaign 1860* (Albany, New York: Weed, Parsons and Company, 1860).

Silliker, Ruth L. (editor), *The Rebel Yell and Yankee Hurrah: The Civil War Journal of a Maine Volunteer* (Camden, Maine: Down East Books, 1985).

Simms, William Gilmore, *The Sack and Destruction of Columbia, South Carolina* (Columbia, South Carolina: Power Press of the Daily Phoenix, 1865).

Simpson, Brooks D. and Berlin, Jean V. (editors), *Sherman's Civil War: Selected Correspondence of William T. Sherman, 1860-1865* (Chapel Hill, North Carolina: University of North Carolina Press, 1999).

Spence, James, "The American Republic: Resurrection Through Dissolution," *Northern British Review*, Number LXXXI, February 1862.

Spence, James, *On the Recognition of the Southern Confederation* (London: Richard Bentley, 1862).

Spence, James, *The American Union: Its Effect on National Character and Policy With an Enquiry Into Secession as a Constitutional Right and the Causes of Disruption* (London: Richard Bentley, 1862).

Stampp, Kenneth M., *The Imperiled Union: Essays on the Background of the Civil War* (New York: Oxford University Press 1980).

Stephens, Alexander H., *A Constitutional View of the War Between the States* (two volumes; Philadelphia, Pennsylvania: National Publishing Company, 1870).

Sumner, Charles, *The Works of Charles Sumner* (fifteen volumes; Boston: Lee and Shepherd, 1875-1883).

Thomas, Benjamin P., *Abraham Lincoln: A Biography* (New York: Alfred A. Knopf, 1952).

Thornbrough, Emma Lou, *The Negro in Indiana: A Study of a Minority* (Indianapolis, Indiana: Indiana Historical Bureau, 1957).

Tocqueville, Alexis de, *Democracy in America* (London: George Allard, 1838).

Trumbull, Lyman, *Speech of Hon. Lyman Trumbull, of Illinois, at a Mass Meeting in Chicago, August 7, 1858* (Washington, D.C.: Buell and Blanchard, Printers, 1858).

Waddell, Gene (editor), *John Bachman: Selected Writings on Science, Race, and Religion* (Athens, Georgia: University of Georgia Press, 2011).

Wallace, William Allen, *The History of Canaan, New Hampshire* (Concord, New Hampshire: The Rumford Press, 1910).

Warshauer, Matthew, *Connecticut in the American Civil War: Slavery, Sacrifice, and Survival* (Middleton, Connecticut: Wesleyan University Press, 2011).

Welles, Gideon, *Diary of Gideon Welles, Secretary of the Navy Under Lincoln and Johnson* (two volumes; Boston: Houghton Mifflin Company, 1911).

Wesley, Charles H., "The Negro's Struggle For Freedom in its Birthplace," *Journal of Negro History*, Volume XXX (1945).

Wheaton, Henry, *Elements of International Law* (Boston: Little, Brown and Company, 1863).

Whiting, William, *The War Powers of the President* (Boston: John L. Shorey, 1862).

Wiley, Earl B., "'Governor' John Greiner and Chase's Bid for the Presidency in 1860," *Ohio State Archaeological and Historical Quarterly*, Number LVIII (1940).

Williams, George W., *History of the Negro Race in America From 1619 to 1880* (two volumes; New York: G. P. Putnam's Sons, 1885).

Williams, T. Harry, *Lincoln and the Radicals* (Madison, Wisconsin: The University of Wisconsin Press, 1941).

Wilson, Woodrow, *A History of the American People* (five volumes; New York: Harper and Brothers, Publishers, 1901).

Yacovone, Donald (editor), *A Voice of Thunder: A Black Soldier's Civil War* (Chicago: University of Illinois Press, 1998).

Other Titles By the Author

America's Caesar: The Decline and Fall of Republican
Government in the United States of America (2014)

State Sovereignty and the Right of Secession: An Historical
and Constitutional Defense of the Southern Position (2015)

Ex Uno Plures: Traditional Southern Presbyterian
Thought on Race Relations (2016)

Intrigue and Invasion: The Economic Background of the
War of 1861-1865 and How the Lincoln Administration
Initiated Hostilities at Fort Sumter (2019)

Northern Aggression and Southern Secession:
A Brief History of Slavery, Taxes, and the War Against the
South, 1861-1865 (2019)